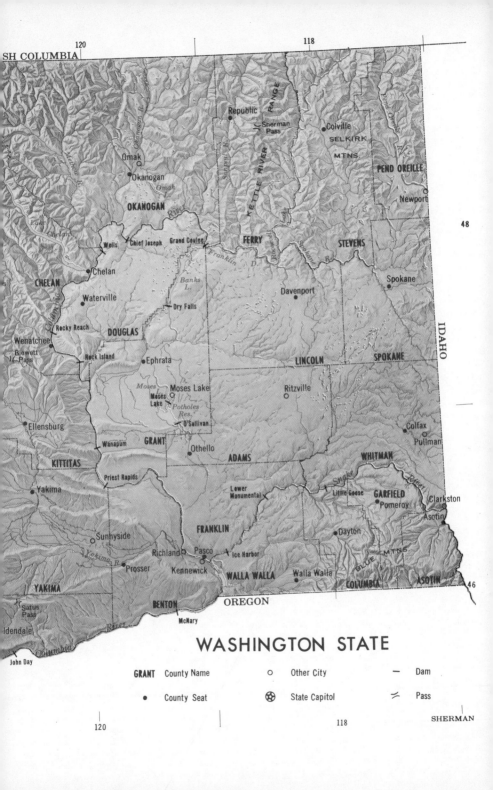

WASHINGTON STATE

GRANT	County Name	○	Other City	—	Dam
●	County Seat	⊗	State Capitol	≿	Pass

Washington State Place Names

James W. Phillips

Washington

State

Place Names

UNIVERSITY OF WASHINGTON PRESS

Seattle & London

To the memory of Edmond S. Meany, professor of history at the University of Washington, whose original works on Washington State history and place name origins served in great measure as the inspiration and source for this book.

Preface

THIS work does not pretend to be a gazetteer of all geographical names in Washington State. It does attempt to be a reasonably comprehensive dictionary of place name meanings that—in my opinion —are of the most importance and interest.

Name selection is based on four primary sources: the federal census compilation of incorporated cities and towns; the 1976 Association of Washington Cities' roster of incorporated municipalities; the United States Postal Service's 1975 directory of post offices; and the decisions of the Washington State Board on Geographic Names. Purposely omitted from the text in the interest of space are obvious self-explanatory or semiduplicating titles (Lake Forest Park, West Richland) and "districts" of communities (Ballard district of Seattle, Hillyard district of Spokane). In contrast to the original volume published in 1971, this edition has less than a dozen communities— one-third of the initial number—with unverified name originations. Furthermore, this updated and expanded volume lists well over five hundred names of features—islands, mountains, rivers, military installations, recreation areas, and other topographical entities—prominent in state geography or history. Emphasis is admittedly and purposely on native, explorer, and pioneer names that give the state its richly varied and educationally interesting heritage.

In many instances, a variety of explanations and apocryphal myths exist as to the origin or evolution of a place name. In all such instances, I have given what is in my opinion the best documented and most logical definition. Although archives have been searched and local contacts made, corrections and clarifications are inevitable (and expected). Hence, readers with additional information on places mentioned or omitted are invited to send documentation to the author in care of the publisher so that future editions can be revised and expanded.

Obviously, in a work of this nature, the author is indebted to a variety of research sources. Professor Edmond S. Meany's 1922 book, *Origin of Washington Place Names,* was a prime reference source, as were the writings of other historians and the archives of newspapers, museums, and historical societies throughout the state. In addition, I could not have written the book without the cooperation and expertise of community officials, postmasters, and "old timers," who submitted to interviews and responded to querying letters. Particular acknowledgment for assistance is due four librarians: Hazel E. Mills of the Washington State Library, Olympia; Phoebe Harris of the Seattle Public Library; Frank L. Green of the Washington State Historical Society, Tacoma; and Bertha N. Stratford of the Seattle Historical Society. In addition, special thanks are due to the staffs of the Seattle Indian Center and tribal offices; to officials of the United States Postal Service; to Gene R. Little, executive secretary, and the regular and associate members of the Washington State Board on Geographic Names (referred to in the text as WSBGN); and to Donald J. Orth, executive secretary of the United States Board on Geographic Names.

Of immeasurable value in this compilation has been the phonetic pronunciation guide compiled by Hugh A. Rundell and issued through the auspices of Washington State University (see p. 167).

JAMES W. PHILLIPS

Seattle, Washington
May 1, 1976

Introduction

WHEN it comes to state names, Washington is unique. It is the only state in the nation to be named after a President, the only one created under the Constitution that departs from the established practice of adapting its name from a local native word, geographical feature, or regional term in common usage. Over the centuries, the Evergreen State has been known by many names. It was part of the region called Alta California by the Spanish, Nova Albion (that is, New England) by Sir Francis Drake, and New Georgia after England's King George III by Captain George Vancouver. It has been variously and chronologically titled Oregon Country, Oregon Territory, Northern Oregon, Washington Territory, and finally Washington State. Even that final designation was initially clouded with alternate suggestions: Tahoma, Columbia, and Washingtonia.

The historical significance—as well as the romance, confusion, and mystery—of its place names extends to every corner of the state. The names reflect the marked influence of the Indian, Spanish, French, and Anglo-American languages. Three waves of professional name-givers left indelible reminders of early exploration— Spanish (San Juan, Orcas, Camano islands); English (Mt. Rainier, Hood Canal, Dungeness); and American (Bainbridge Island, Mt. Constitution, Elliott Bay). Some of the early trappers and settlers retained or attached—albeit phonetically spelled or misspelled—Indian terms (Okanogan, Hamma Hamma, Snohomish). Others, with a touch of nostalgia, duplicated names from the Old Country (Bingen, Kent, Geneva), while still other pioneers selected names that indicated their grandiose dreams (Opportunity, Acme, Paradise).

State names honor first homesteaders, civic leaders, and business tycoons. Towns were named for women (La Conner, Ellensburg, Zillah, Mabton), for Biblical terms (Eglon, Ephrata), and for businesses (Carnation, Du Pont). Some site names are misspellings (Algona, Edmonds), others are cases of mistaken identity (Magnolia Bluff, Cypress Island), and still others were named with a touch of wry wit (Felida, Puyallup).

Names for budding communities were often chosen by part-time, self-nominated local postmasters for reasons known—or significant —only to themselves. Minions of the Postmaster General in the far distant national capital also arbitrarily assigned names for no apparent reason other than to expedite a post office application. Professional land developers conjured up town titles with melodious sales appeal to stimulate an influx of settlers. However, as a group, the most prolific place namers were the railroads, which were faced with the awesome task of identifying every station, section house, siding, and whistle stop along the thousands of miles of track laid in the latter decades of the nineteenth century. Some duplicated the prosaic and festooned the countryside with inappropriate names copied from other sections of the country; a few exercised imagination. One railroad official who took his name-bestowing duties seriously was H. R. Williams, vice president of the Milwaukee line, who established a set of rules to assure the suitability of a name before it was officially approved: one which was reasonably short, easily spelled, pleasant sounding, and which, when called, written, or telegraphed, would not be confused with another name in the vicinity or on the company's trackage. Judiciously exercising his criteria, Williams named thirty-two stations in Washington. Among them were Horlick after the malted drink, Warden to honor a stockholder, Ralston after the health food, Revere for the patriot equestrian, Whittier for the poet, Pandora for the infamous box, Marcellus for an easterner he once met, and Beverly, Boylston, and Malden for towns in Massachusetts.

The following pages briefly explain the story behind the place names in Washington State. The text also points up our debt to the sense of discrimination demonstrated by the founding fathers in selecting names. Had they not rejected or modified a large number of Indian words, local geography would be dotted with guttural tongue-twisters: Whulge instead of Puget Sound; Duwamps, Chebaulip, and Stitchas for, respectively, Seattle, Tacoma, and Olympia; and a variation of Lewis and Clark's Skeetsomish would apply to Spokane.

Conversely, had words of Indian derivation not been adopted and euphonically adapted, many pleasant-sounding places would be known by a host of improbable titles: Commencement City in lieu of Tacoma; Steptoeville for Walla Walla; Slaughter instead of Kitsap County. Issaquah might be called by any of four former names: Gilman, Olney, Englewood, or Squak. Alki Point could have retained two officially charted navy names—Battery Point or Point Roberts—and Cle Elum would be Cle Alum to suit the dictates of the railroad telegraphy code.

The Indian names perpetuated in the state's geography are as diversified in origin as those implanted by the white men, as the Indians native to the area represented a variety of separate tribes or language families (Salishan, Shahaptian, Shapwailutan, Athapascan, Wakashan, Chinookan). It is estimated by philologists that as many as forty different languages and distinct dialects were spoken by local aborigines. To overcome this handicap, many of the Indians, prior to the arrival of the white man, adopted as a means of commerce a simplified version of Chinookan, the language of the powerful tribe of traders that resided along the lower reaches of the Columbia River.

With the advent of the white man, this basic language blossomed into a full-fledged *lingua franca,* utilized by all Indians and white men of the period. Known as the Chinook jargon, it was based primarily on the Chinookan tongue, but included words from all the languages of all the peoples who used it. It was strongly influenced by the French-Canadian trappers and *voyageurs* of Hudson's Bay Company, by the English "King George tillikums," and by the American "Bostonmen."

The different native dialects, coupled with the free-style spelling employed by the whites, resulted in a wide range of spellings—and even definitions—of present place names. Conversion from Indian to French to English by well-meaning, but often uneducated, place-namers and history recorders, further compounded the problem. Yet the native names live on as an integral and meaningful part of the landscape.

Washington's place names are to a great measure the reflection of its exploration and settlement. Hence, to add meaning to the stories of its names, a short—oversimplified—recounting of the state's history is in order.

Sir Francis Drake sailed the *Golden Hind* along the Pacific coast shores, perhaps, though unlikely, as far north as the Washington coast in 1579. He was followed, in fact or in myth, by a Greek named Apostolos Valerianos who, under the pseudonym Juan de Fuca, sailed Pacific waters in 1592 for the Spanish viceroy of Mexico. In his retirement years in Europe, the navigator spun a tale of finding the Strait of Anian. English geographer Michael Lok accepted the alleged discovery and entered it on his charts, thus rekindling adventurous sea captains' search for the nonexistent Northwest Passage.

The name-giving business really began in 1774 when Juan Perez sailed close to Washington shores en route from Mexico to Alaska. He spotted a majestic, snow-capped mountain and named it El Cerro de la Santa Rosalia, and thus Mt. Olympus became the first geographical feature in the state to be given a name. The following year, two more Spanish captains, Juan Francisco de la Bodega y Quadra and Bruno Heceta, explored the coast and bestowed names.

In 1778, England's famed Captain James Cook, en route from the

Sandwich (Hawaiian) Islands to Vancouver Island (with explorer-to-be of Washington waters, George Vancouver, in his crew), missed Juan de Fuca's sought-after strait, but named Cape Flattery. He also discovered the value the Chinese placed on sea-otter skins, which were in plentiful supply in the Pacific Northwest.

In the interest of territorial acquisition and dollars from the lucrative sea-otter fur trade with China, the exploration rush to Washington via water was under way. In 1787, England's Charles W. Barclay found the entrance of a great strait and named it "after its original discoverer, Juan de Fuca." Englishman John Meares raised Washington's coast in 1788 and renamed Mt. Olympus. Spain's Francisco de Eliza explored the state's northern waters in 1791; American Robert Gray discovered and named the Columbia River in 1792; English explorer Captain George Vancouver sailed Puget Sound in 1792. And, finally, the most prolific namer of all explorers, Lieutenant Charles Wilkes of the United States Navy, commanded an exploration of the region's inland waters and adjacent land in 1841. Formally titled the United States Exploring Expedition of 1838–42, but more commonly called the Wilkes Expedition, it was the forerunner of a series of detailed surveys by government agencies.

Each of the explorers affixed names to the land for a variety of reasons—after crew members, because of topographical features, as the location of a particular occurrence. Being politically wise or patriotically inclined, these professionals frequently utilized the names of patrons, sponsors, or superiors. For example, Eliza's patron was Señor Don Juan Vicente de Güemes Pacheco Padilla Horcasitas y Aguayo, Conde de Revilla Gigedo, who is liberally honored in our geography: Orcas Island, Guemes Island, Padilla Bay. When this viceroy of Mexico was not the name source, Eliza and his fellow naval captains resorted to saints' names, each other's names, and descriptive Spanish terms of a nautical flavor.

Vancouver frequently followed suit in the name-dropping game, as evidenced by his use of the names of Lord Samuel Hood, Admiral Peter Rainier, and Sir William Bellingham, who were all highly placed in the British Admiralty. While many of the place names endowed by Vancouver honor British admirals who gained their fame and fortune by defeating American forces in the Revolutionary War, he did name some sites for such nonfoes as Lieutenant Peter Puget and Master Joseph Whidbey of his crew.

A dedicated patriot and an unabashed hero worshiper, Wilkes attempted to convert the San Juan Islands into the Navy Archipelago by affixing the names of naval officers and ships of the War of 1812: San Juan to Rodgers Island for John Rodgers, captain of the frigate U.S.S. *President*; Orcas to Hull Island for Commodore Isaac Hull of the U.S.S. *Constitution*. When he ran out of heroes, he switched to his own peers and to members of his expedition force. Puget Sound is replete with the namesakes of Wilkes's men—major waterways for commissioned officers and scientists, lesser points for petty officers—but no spot in the state bears his own name.

The double naming was not necessarily intentional. Because of difficulties of communication during that era, seafarers and trail blazers of one nation often were unaware of the travels and mapping of explorers of other countries. Admittedly, however, the rights of possession by exploration and by settlement were often prime motives for bestowing nationalistic names. Either by accident or by intent, there was overlap. The second largest island of the San Juan Group was an excellent example—San Juan to the Spanish, Bellevue to Hudson's Bay Company, and Rodgers Island to Wilkes.

For a while official maps carried conflicting or multiple names for many sites. The confusion was resolved to a great degree in 1847 by issuance and inter-nation circulation of charts prepared by Captain Henry Kellett of the British Admiralty. The new charts restored many of the original Spanish names, replaced obscure names with those in general use, and in some instances moved names with pedigreed heritages that had been overshadowed in local usage to nearby locations to preserve historical flavor. While Kellett is credited with making order of chaos, his changes perpetuated British names at the expense of many American titles. He replaced many United States names by arbitrarily relocating Spanish names that conflicted with those of British origin.

While seafarers were busy exploring and naming, inroads deep within the present state borders were being made by land travelers —explorers, trappers, missionaries, and prospectors. These men, and the homesteaders who followed them, also had a penchant for identifying. Captains Meriwether Lewis and William Clark mapped their way down the Columbia River in 1805–6. Britain's Northwest Fur Company established Spokane House—the first white settlement within the state—in 1810. The following year, John Jacob Astor's Pacific Fur Company established a trading post near the mouth of the Columbia River and a fort in the Okanogan country. In 1825, Hudson's Bay Company—staffed by Britishers, French-Canadian trappers, and Hawaiian Islanders—set up Fort Vancouver.

Marcus Whitman and H. H. Spalding, accompanied by their wives, opened a mission near Walla Walla in 1836. Catholic Fathers Francis N. Blanchet and Modeste Demers traveled the country in 1838. The influx of settlers of all nationalities continued as Americans vied with the British for dominance in the Oregon Country. The first Americans settled in Tumwater, heart of the British-controlled region, in 1845. The following year, the English-American boundary dispute was settled; the region from the Columbia River north to the present Canadian border officially became part of the United States, and the population boom began.

In eastern Washington, trappers gave way to prospectors, who, in turn, were replaced by (or voluntarily changed into) ranchers and orchardists. Shipping, logging, and farming sparked development west of the Cascades, and 1851–52 saw the arrival of the founding fathers of Port Townsend, Seattle, Tacoma, and Bellingham. By 1853, Washington was a separate territory with a white population of nearly 4,000; by 1889, when it became a state, the population had jumped to 337,232. And it was thus that the ever-continuing naming in Washington began.

Pronunciation Guide

Accented syllables appear in capital letters (Island = EYE-luhnd), un-accented syllables in lower case.

AY	GREY, BAY, SALE
A	CAT, RAN
AH	TOP
AW	BOUGHT, SAW
AIR	CARE, FAIR
EE	SEE, TREAT
E	BET, SAID
ER	CURVE, SMIRK
EYE	SIGHT, FLY
EEUH	MANIA
I	BIT
IR	PIERCE
OH	SEW, GO
OW	OUT, ROUND, ALLOW
OO	BOOT, SUIT, ROOF
<u>OO</u>	FOOT, SHOULD, BUSH
OI	BOY, POINT
OR	DOOR, BOARD
YOO	CUE, MENU
UH	CUP, AGAIN, TOUGH
G	GUN
J	JUNK
S	SALARY, CELERY
K	KICK, CAKE

Washington State Place Names

Aberdeen (Grays Harbor). Platted in 1884 on the Samuel Benn homestead between the Chehalis and Wishkah rivers at the eastern end of Grays Harbor, the city is the namesake of Aberdeen, Scotland. Prompted by the presence of the Aberdeen Packing Co. on Benn's waterfront, Mrs. James B. Stewart suggested that the town be called after her native city: "Being the firm name of the cannery there and to our ears quite pleasing." Finnish-born cannery owner B. A. Seaborg, who had originally named his company to capitalize on the Scottish city's prominence in the fisheries world, seconded the idea and contended that the name was most appropriate, as the Gaelic word meant "the meeting of two rivers."

Acme (Whatcom). Named by resident George Parls in 1887 after a local church's newly received Acme hymn book. A Greek word, *acme* means "culmination" or "top or highest point."

Adams, Mt. (Yakima). The Indians called it Pahto, the name of a legendary brave who was turned into a mountain by a wrathful god. In 1830–43 there were efforts to change the name of the Cascades to the Presidents' Range and to rename major peaks for individual presidents. Among the proposed new titles, St. Helens would become Washington, Baker would be Tyler, Rainier would honor Harrison, and Olympus would be Van Buren. In the process, un-

3

named Adams acquired the name of the second United States President.

Adams County; 1,895 sq. mi.; 16th in size; seat: Ritzville. Formation authorized by territorial legislature enactment of 28 November 1883. The name honors John Adams, second United States President.

Addy (Stevens). Originally a Swiss dairy community, the town was given in 1890 the nickname of his wife, Adeline, by E. S. Dudrey, storekeeper and first postmaster.

Admiralty Inlet. The waterway that connects the Strait of Juan de Fuca with Puget Sound was named by Vancouver to honor his ultimate commanders, the Board of Admiralty that supervised the royal navy of Great Britain.

Adna (Lewis). An early settler named Browning originally called the town Willoway after his wife's favorite saying: "Where there's a will, there's a way." In 1892 the railroad changed the name to Pamona to distinguish it from Willapa townsite. Discovery in 1894 of a Pamona post office east of the Cascade Mountains resulted in the railway superintendent's renaming the town for a member of his family—Adna Marian.

Aeneas, EE-nee-uhs (Okanogan). Named for a local Indian chief who gained fame as a government guide.

Agate Pass (Kitsap). Named by Wilkes for the expedition's artist, Alfred T. Agate.

Agnew (Clallam). Community between Sequim and Port Angeles named for 1889 pioneer Charles Agnew. It is a consolidation of the former towns of Reeveton and Lindsay.

Ahtanum Creek, uh-TEN-uhm (Yakima). Stream bordering the edge of the Yakima Indian Reservation derives its name from *Ahtanumlema,* the name of an Indian band that once lived along the creek. The term literally translates to "people of the water by the long hill." St. Joseph's Catholic Mission was the first structure where the small community now stands.

Ainsworth (Franklin). A railroad junction named in honor of early day railroader J. C. Ainsworth.

Airway Heights (Spokane). So named because of its proximity to the two airfields on the west side of Spokane.

Ajlune, AJ-loon (Lewis). Named by the first postmaster, Ghosn Ghasn, for his birthplace in Lebanon.

Alava, Cape, AH-lah-vuh, uh-LAH-vuh (Clallam). The western-most point in the original 48 states was named for José Manuel de Alava, commissioner for Spain at the Nootka Convention of 1790. Because of mud slides that covered a succession of Makah Indian villages, the locality has proven to be a rich archeological find—an American Pompeii—yielding artifacts at least 2,500 years old. [*See* Neah Bay; Ozette, Lake; Tatoosh Island.]

Albion (Whitman). Changed from the original name of Guy in 1901 at the insistence of a local resident of English extraction to honor early explorations by the British—particularly Sir Francis Drake, who sailed the Pacific Northwest coast in 1579 and named the region Nova Albion, "New England."

Alden Point (San Juan). Both the western tip of Patos Island and Alden Bank east of the island (but in Whatcom County) were named—at different times—for the same man: Lt. Cmdr. James Alden, who twice served in Puget Sound waters. He first served with Wilkes in 1841. The second time was during the Indian Wars of 1855-56, when he diverted his steamer *Active* from routine hy-drographic survey duties to fight the battle of Seattle.

Alder (Pierce). Named in 1902 for a grove of alder trees where the town is located. Railroad name: New Reliance.

Alderdale (Klickitat). Named by Western Investment Co. at the time the town was platted because of its location at the mouth of Alder Creek.

Alderton (Pierce). Named by homesteader Orson Annis for the piles of alder cordwood stacked alongside the Northern Pacific Railroad tracks for use as engine fuel.

Algona, al-GOH-nah (King). Original title of Valley City was rejected by the post office as a duplication of a community name already existing in the state. A town meeting 10 February 1910 selected the Indian word *algoma,* meaning "valley of flowers." Postal authorities accepted the name, but misspelled it in official records. Oddly, the city's name occurs frequently elsewhere in the United States as a coined term for an area in Canada bordering Lakes Superior and Huron. The usage stems from *al,* from the tribal name Algonquin, and the Algonquin word *goma,* meaning "lake."

Alki Point, AL-keye (King). The southwestern shore of Elliott Bay, where the founding fathers of Seattle—the Arthur Denny party of 12 adults and 12 children—first settled on 13 November 1851. The Indians had called the spot Ma-que-buck or Me-kwa-mooks. Wilkes had mapped it as Point Roberts, presumably to honor one (or all) of four men in his force with that surname. However, the visionary pioneers called their new home New York, and later, in trepidation at its slow growth, added a hyphen and the Chinook jargon word *alki,* meaning "by and by." In 1856, the U.S. Coast Survey officially charted it as Battery Point for its potential as a fortification site. However, common usage prevailed, and all names except Alki were eventually dropped.

Allan Island (Skagit). Despite substitution of an *a* for the final *e,* the island was named by Wilkes in honor of Capt. William Henry Allen, who was killed aboard the *Argus* while engaging the British brig *Pelican* in the War of 1812. To intensify the honor, Wilkes named the waters between Allan and Fidalgo islands as Argus Bay. However, that name has been replaced by Burrows Bay, which honors another of Wilkes's naval heroes. [*See* Burrows Island.]

Allen (Skagit). Shingle mill operated by Allen, Roray, and Sanburn was the name source for the Samish River community.

Allison (Pierce). Named for John B. Allison, logging-camp operator in the area, *circa* 1900.

Allyn (Mason). Named for Judge Frank Allyn of Tacoma, who was involved in the formation of the town, *circa* 1889.

Almira, al-MEYE-ruh (Lincoln). Named in 1889 after Almira Davis, wife of Charles C. Davis, the town's first merchant.

Almota, al-MOH-tuh (Whitman). Site of an Indian village where Lewis and Clark camped on 11 October 1805, the name is derived from the Nez Perce term *alla motin,* meaning "torchlight fishing."

Aloha, a-LOH-hah (Grays Harbor). Town name was adopted from the Hawaiian word for love, a word used as a greeting or farewell.

Alstown, AWL-stuhn (Douglas). Named in honor of civil engineer Al Rogers of Waterville, a local civic leader and one-time regent of the University of Washington.

Altoona (Wahkiakum). Founded in 1910 as site of a fish cannery, the community was named after Altona, Germany, major fish-processing city on the Elbe River.

Amanda Park (Grays Harbor). Named for the wife of Joseph J. Southard, cofounder of a store–motel–private-park complex in 1926.

Amber (Spokane). The original name of Calvert, after one of the area's first settlers, was changed to coincide with the name of an existing post office on an adjacent homestead.

Amboy, AM-boy (Clark). Post office established 19 July 1886 by mill operator Amos M. Ball, who selected the town name from a list provided by the Post Office Department.

American Lake (Pierce). Named in sequence as Richmond, Gordon, Tolmie, and American Lake. The present name resulted from the influx of American homesteaders to the lake area, in contrast to British population at nearby Fort Nisqually.

Anacortes, an-uh-KOR-tis (Skagit). Fidalgo Island's main city changed names in 1876: from Ship Harbor to Anacortes. The change was wrought by Amos Bowman, town platter and pro-moter, who gave it a Spanish-sounding version of his wife's maiden name—Anna Curtis—so that it would better fit its setting and his real estate development dreams.

Anatone, AN-uh-tohn (Asotin). For this busy trading post on the gold trail of the 1860s, the whites simply adopted the Indian name for the site. According to legend, the name was originally that of an Indian woman who once lived in the area.

Anderson Island (Pierce). Named in 1841 by Wilkes for Alexander Canfield Anderson, chief trader for Hudson's Bay Co. at Fort Nisqually. It was subsequently, but futilely, given two other names: Fisgard Island for the British frigate *Fisgard* that sailed Puget Sound waters, 1844–47, and Wallace Island for Leander C. Wallace, who was killed in the Snoqualmie Indian attack on Fort Nisqually in 1849. [*See* McNeil Island.]

Annas Bay (Mason). Charted by Wilkes as Anna's Bay, but subsequent maps dropped the apostrophe.

Appledale (Douglas). Former town was so named in 1909 when it was established as a railroad apple-shipping center.

Appleton (Klickitat). So named because it was an apple-growing center.

Appleyard (Chelan). Railroad station name for South Wenatchee. It was established as the terminal yard or collection point for the Great Northern's shipment of apples from "The Apple Capital of the World" to national markets.

Ardenvoir, AHR-duhn-vawr (Chelan). Named after Ardenvoir Harris, the "son" in C. A. Harris and Son, Inc., local sawmill operation.

Ariel, AIR-ee-uhl (Cowlitz). Named for Ariel Chitty, son of the first postmaster. The town's name literally means "lion of God" and is a title applied to Jerusalem in the Old Testament. Subsequent namesakes include a character in Shakespeare's *The Tempest,* a satellite of the planet Uranus, and a small boat used for shore explorations by the Wilkes Expedition.

Arletta, ahr-LE-tuh (Pierce). Name was coined from the first names of Arla and Letty Powell, daughters of the lower Kitsap Peninsula community's first postmaster.

Arlington (Snohomish). Originally called The Forks, denoting a logging settlement at the confluence of the north and south forks of the Stillaguamish River, the city is the consolidation of two competitive townsites: Haller City, platted in 1883, and Arlington, developed by railroad contractors in 1890. Haller City was named by Maurice Haller to honor his father, Maj. Granville O. Haller, who served prominently in the Indian Wars. Arlington, an oft-repeated geographic name (including that of the national cemetery in Virginia, the former estate of Robert E. Lee), stems from Lord Henry Arlington, cabinet minister to Charles II of England.

Artic (Grays Harbor). Arta was the name on the application for a post office at this site in the 1880s. The name was to honor Mrs. Arta Saunders, wife of the town founder. The writing was sloppy and postal authorities misread the final *a* as *ic,* hence, the desired name was converted to a geographically inappropriate mispelling of the word "arctic."

Ashford (Pierce). Honors town founder, Walter A. Ashford.

Asotin, uh-SOH-tin (Asotin). Two settlements, Asotin and Asotin City, started within one-half mile of each other in the early 1870s, but merged into a single community within a decade. When the county was organized in 1883, it adopted the same name and the town as its seat.

Asotin County; 627 sq. mi.; 35th in size; seat: Asotin. Nez Perce Indian word meaning "eel creek," as numerous eels were caught at the point where Asotin Creek joins the Snake River.

Attalia, a-TAL-liuh (Walla Walla). Former farming center and irrigation project headquarters was named for a hamlet in Italy in 1906 by the wife of developer V. K. Loose of Seattle.

Auburn, AW-burn (King). Platted in 1886 by Dr. Levi W. Ballard as Slaughter in honor of Lt. William A. Slaughter, who was killed in the Indian War of 1855–56. The morbidity of the name per se offended residents (the hotel, for example, was called the Slaughter House), and they petitioned the state legislature for a change in 1893. The city was renamed after Auburn, N.Y.—another major hop-farming center—which had been named in 1805 for a line in an Oliver Goldsmith poem reading: "Sweet Auburn! loveliest village of the plain."

Ault Field (Island). Airfield at Whidbey Island Naval Air Station was named for Cmdr. William B. Ault, killed in air combat in the Battle of the Coral Sea in 1942, the year the airstrip was established.

Avon (Skagit). Founded in 1882 as a "no saloons" temperance town, the name was purportedly selected to "honor the birthplace of William Shakespeare."

Azwell, AZ-well (Chelan). Originally called Wells, the town was renamed in 1936 in honor of A. Z. Wells, prominent Wenatchee merchant who had large orchard holdings around the community.

---

b

Badger (Benton). A spring near the townsite flowed from one of the many badger holes in the area, so it was called Badger Flats by the first settlers.

Bainbridge Island (Kitsap). Named by Wilkes for Commodore William Bainbridge, naval captain in both the war with Tripoli and the War of 1812. He is particularly remembered as one of two captains who, by urging "let us meet the foe at sea," persuaded President James Madison to abandon the 1812 plan to anchor, demast, and use the navy's seven frigates as harbor batteries. His greatest victory was as captain of the *Constitution,* when, though wounded, he defeated the superior British *Java.* A close personal friend of Stephen Decatur, he served the navy's "firebrand" as second in Decatur's fatal duel. [*See* Decatur Island.]

Baker, Mt. (Whatcom). Indian name for the mountain varied from tribe to tribe, but two of the most consistently used were the Nooksaks' Koma Kulshan, for "white, steep mountain," and the Lummis' Kulshan, meaning "shot at the point," apparently in reference to early eruption that shattered the once conical peak of the now dormant volcano. In 1790 the Spanish explorer Manuel Quimper named the peak La Montana del Carmelo, which poetically translates to "Great White Watcher." The present name was assigned 30 April 1792 by Vancouver to honor Lt. Joseph Baker, first Englishman to sight the mountain.

Bakers Bay (Pacific). Named by the Vancouver Expedition for Capt. James Baker of the American schooner *Jenny,* which they found anchored there.

Ballinger, Lake (Snohomish). In early 1900, Judge Richard A. Ballinger (Seattle mayor, president of the Alaska-Yukon-Pacific Exposition, Secretary of the Interior under Taft) acquired the lake and adjacent land and named it for his father, Col. R. H. Ballinger, former Civil War officer who had studied law in Abraham Lincoln's Springfield office.

Bangor, BANG-gawr (Kitsap). Now a U.S. naval ammunition depot, the site was initially called Three Spits because of sand spits jutting into Hood Canal. Subsequently it was known as Carlston, one of two so-named communities in the county. When the town was officially platted in 1890, it was named Bangor, presumably by former New Englanders after the similarly titled city in Maine, which, in turn, is the namesake of a city in Wales.

Barberton (Clark). Named in 1892 for postmaster Edwin H. Barber.

Bare Island (San Juan). So named because of its scant vegetation. [*See* Skipjack Island.]

Baring (King). Established as a lumber center on the Great Northern Railroad line, the town was platted 10 June 1901 and named for nearby Mt. Baring.

Barnes Island (San Juan). Both Barnes and nearby Clark Island were named by Wilkes to honor naval heroes of the War of 1812. [*See* Clark Island.]

Battle Ground (Clark). Named by A. H. Richter, who established a store in 1886 and platted the town in 1902 at the site of a skirmish between troops from Fort Vancouver and Indian horse thieves in the mid-1800s.

Battleship Island (San Juan). So named because its silhouette resembles that of a battleship.

Bay Center (Pacific). So named because it is the midway point on the east shore of Willapa Bay. Situated at the tip of a triangular peninsula, the town is virtually the geographic center of the bay.

Bazalgette Point, BAZ-al-get-ee (San Juan). Southern point of Roche Harbor was named in 1868 by Capt. Daniel Pender of the royal navy to honor British Army Capt. George Bazalgette, commander of the British camp near Garrison Bay, San Juan Island, 1860–67, during the boundary dispute.

Beaux Arts, BOHZ-ARTZ (King). A village patterned after the garden villages of England was founded by the Beaux Arts Society in 1908. One of the group organizers was painter Sidney Lawrence, famed for Alaskan landscapes and marine subjects. Intended to be the arts and crafts center of the Pacific Northwest, the community is now a lakeside residential area west of Bellevue.

Beaver (Clallam). The logging community takes its name from nearby Beaver Creek and lake which, in turn, were named for the proliferation of beaver in the area when it was settled by Martin Kopanski in 1891.

Belfair (Mason). To avoid duplication with a proliferation of towns called Clifton, the Postmaster-General requested renaming in 1925. Mrs. Murray, postmistress 1914–25, submitted Belfair, which was mentioned in a book entitled *St. Almo* that she was then reading.

Belfast (Skagit). Name suggested by William Gilmore, pioneer merchant at nearby Edison, to honor his home town in Ireland.

Bellevue (King). A French term meaning "beautiful view" was selected by a post office naming committee in the early 1880s, purportedly because of the community's excellent view toward the Olympic Mountains.

Bellevue Point (San Juan). Situated on the southwestern shore of San Juan Island, the point reflects the early British name for San

Juan Island. Hudson's Bay Co. operated Bellevue Farm on the island, and the early English charts originally applied the name to the entire island.

Bellingham (Whatcom). In the half-century following settlement of the Bellingham Bay area there were several adjacent communities on the bay shore. At different times, as separate or merged entities, the towns were known as Whatcom, Sehome, New Whatcom, Pattle's Point, Unionville, (Old) Bellingham, and Fairhaven. In 1904 they consolidated under the Bellingham city charter and became the county seat.

Bellingham Bay (Whatcom). The bay, like the town on its shore, also had a plethora of names: Gulf of Gaston, Bellingham Bay, Gaston Bay, and Ballsam Bay. Eliza, who was the first known white man to enter the bay, called it Gulf of Gaston in 1791. The following year it was surveyed by Joseph Whidbey of the expedition under Vancouver's command. The latter gave it the English name of Bellingham after Sir William Bellingham, controller of the British Navy's storekeeper account, who personally checked Vancouver's supplies prior to the captain's departure from England in April 1791.

Bellingham Channel (Skagit). The waterway between Guemes and Cypress islands was called Tut-segh by the Indians and Canal de Guemes by Eliza. Its present name, taken from Bellingham Bay, was assigned by the U.S. Coast Survey in 1853.

Belmont (Whitman). Name source unverified.

Benge, BENJ (Adams). Named for Frank Benge, who donated the townsite when the railroad cut through his homestead in 1907.

Benton City (Benton). Actual source of this name's origin is vague. One version suggests that railroad executives bestowed it as a tie in to the county name. Another that it honors Benton C. Grosscup, who was active in the separation of Benton County from Yakima County. Whatever the reason, the end result was an improvement, as the townsite was initially platted by J. G. Giezentanner, postmaster of nearby Kiona, who assigned it his own name.

Benton County; 1,738 sq. mi.; 21st in size; seat: Prosser. Named in 1905 in honor of Missouri Senator Thomas H. Benton, who was favorable to pro-western legislation. The first to serve 30 years in the U.S. Senate, he was nicknamed "Old Bullion" because he opposed paper currency. He championed the pony express, transcontinental telegraph, and highways to the interior. McKinley and Riverside were alternate names proposed for the county formed from the eastern portions of Yakima and Klickitat counties.

Ben Ure Island, BEN ER (Island). The 10.9-acre island was purchased on 20 May 1908 from the federal government by Benjamin Ure, who subdivided it into estate-size tracts.

Beverly (Grant). Named by H. R. Williams, vice president of the Milwaukee Railroad, after a similarly named town in Massachusetts.

Bickelton (Klickitat). Named for Charles N. Bickle, first storekeeper and postmaster, who settled at the townsite in 1879.

Big Lake (Skagit). Descriptive name for a lake east of Mount Vernon that was initially known as Delacey's after an early settler.

Bingen, BIN-jin (Klickitat). The town was laid out by P. J. Suksdorf in 1892 and named after Bingen-on-the-Rhine because the town's location on the Columbia River was reminiscent of the German town's position on the Rhine River.

Birch Bay (Whatcom). The Indians called the spot Tsan-wuch, but Vancouver chose its present name because of the abundance of black birch trees along the shore. Vancouver used the bay as an anchorage in June 1792 for the launching of his small-boat exploration crews.

Birdsview (Skagit). Name derived in 1880 from that of the first postmaster, Birdsey D. Minkler.

Black Diamond (King). Town derived its name from the Black Diamond Coal Co. of California, which opened coal mines in the area in the early 1880s.

Blaine (Whatcom). The "Peace Arch City" at the United States–

Canadian border was platted in 1884 as Concord, but on 23 April 1885 staunch Republican residents renamed it in honor of James C. Blaine, secretary of state under Republican President James A. Garfield and the unsuccessful Republican candidate for President in 1884.

Blake Island (Kitsap). A state marine park at the north entrance of Colvos Passage, the island was named by Wilkes after George Smith Blake, commanding officer of the U.S. Coast Survey, 1837–48. It is the presumed birthplace of Chief Seattle. [*See* Suquamish.]

Blakely Island (San Juan). Named by Wilkes to honor Johnston Blakely, commander of the sloop-of-war *Wasp* during the War of 1812. After numerous daring exploits, including capture of the *Reindeer* for which Congress voted him a gold medal, Blakely's ship and entire crew mysteriously vanished at sea.

Blanchard (Skagit). Founded by and named for George B. Blanchard *circa* 1885. To avoid duplication of post office designations, the town was renamed Fravel after another pioneer family, but the present name was re-established by vote when the other Blanchard post office was discontinued.

Blewett Pass, BLOO-et (Chelan). The pass through the Wenatchee Mountains at the headwaters of Swauk and Peshastin creeks was once the site of the gold-mining town of Blewett. Named for Edward Blewett, who, with Horace Henry of Seattle, was instrumental in development of the district.

Blockhouse (Klickitat). During the Indian Wars, Maj. Granville O. Haller built a fort—an eight-foot-high stockade and two-story blockhouse—on the military road between The Dalles and Fort Simcoe. After five years' occupation by the U.S. Cavalry, the post was abandoned and in 1872 became a private dwelling and post office.

Bluecreek (Stevens). Name source of the Colville River community is unverified. A prosperous sawmill and mining center, *circa* 1890, the town was established as the Blue Creek railroad station.

Blueslide (Pend Oreille). Logging town established in 1906 and named for a nearby hill of bluish-colored clay subject to landslides during rains.

Bluestem (Lincoln). Name was adopted from a variety of wheat grown in the area.

Blyn (Clallam). Named for mill operator Marshall Blinn, who founded Seabeck.

Bogachiel River, BOH-guh-sheel (Clallam). The name is an Indian word meaning "muddy waters." [*See* Quillayute River.]

Boistfort, BOIST-fort (Lewis). Rural community carries an anglicized spelling of two French words—*bois,* meaning "forest," and *fort,* meaning "strong"—affixed to the then heavily forested prairie by former Hudson's Bay Co. employee, Pierre Charles. His given name was, through misunderstanding, the source for the town name of nearby Pe Ell. [*See* Pe Ell.]

Bonneville Dam, BAHN-uh-vil (Skamania). The dam across the Columbia River between North Bonneville, Wash., and Bonneville, Ore., was completed in 1937 and honors Gen. Benjamin Louis Eulalie de Bonneville of the U.S. Army. Born in Paris, France, and a graduate of West Point, Bonneville served in both the Mexican and Civil wars, and, as a captain, extensively explored the Pacific Northwest, 1832–35. Other geographic points honoring him include a county in Oregon, a mountain in Wyoming, and the famed auto-racing salt flats in Utah.

Bonney Lake (Pierce). Situated on the shore of a lake named for an early homesteader, the town was platted in 1947 by Kenneth Simmons, who purchased the lake and 1,000 adjacent acres for the specific purpose of founding the community.

Booker, Mt. (Chelan). Named in 1904 to honor Booker T. Washington at the suggestion of landscape painter Mrs. F. R. Hill of Tacoma, who, on painting the mountain, found it was unofficially titled No Name Peak.

Bossburg (Stevens). Former silver-mining center was named in 1892 for townsite owners C. S. Boss and John Berg.

Boston Harbor (Thurston). Named by Seattle real estate agent C. D. Hillman, who platted and promoted the Dofflemyer donation claim at the Dofflemyer Point entrance to Budd Inlet.

Bothell, BAH-thuhl (King). Named for the David C. Bothell family, which established a shingle mill there in 1886 and platted the town in 1888.

Boundary Bay (Whatcom). The bay is bordered on the east and west by United States soil—Point Roberts and the mainland of Whatcom County—and on the north by British Columbia. So named by the U.S. Coast Survey as it is bisected by the United States–Canadian border, the forty-ninth parallel.

Bow, BOH (Skagit). Originally known as Brownsville after William J. Brown, who homesteaded the townsite in 1869. Advent of the railroad resulted in a population boom and the need for a post office. In deference to the growth brought about by the railroad, Brown suggested the new name of Bow, after the large railway station in London, England—which, in turn, was named for the bow or poplar tree.

Boyds (Ferry). The family name of early settlers in the area.

Brady (Grays Harbor). Named for John Brady, who settled on the Satsop River in 1853 and served as one of the country's first three commissioners in 1854.

Breidablick, BREYED-a-blik (Kitsap). Settled by Scandinavians, the name is from Norse mythology and translates "broad view."

Bremerton, BREM-er-tuhn (Kitsap). Named for William Bremer, a German immigrant and early Washington Territory pioneer, who is regarded as the city's founder.

Brewster (Okanogan). Named in 1896 for the pronunciation rather than the actual spelling of the name of homesteader John Bruster.

Bridgeport (Douglas). Originally called Westfield, the Columbia River steamboat landing was renamed for their Connecticut home in 1891 by railroad surveyors who promoted the townsite.

Brier, BREYE-er (Snohomish). Township adopted the name of the roadway that bisected the community.

Brinnon (Jefferson). Named for early settler Ewell P. Brinnon.

Brooklyn (Pacific). Arbitrarily named by U.S. postal officials.

Brothers, The (Jefferson). Named by Capt. George Davidson of the U.S. Coast Survey in 1856 for members of the Fauntleroy family. [*See* Fauntleroy Cove.]

Broughton Reach (Skamania). The 17-mile-long section of the Columbia River was named jointly in 1975 by the Washington and Oregon geographic place name boards to honor the Vancouver expedition's Lt. William Broughton, commander of the tender *Chatham,* as the first white man to travel as far upstream as the mouth of the Willamette River.

Brown Island (San Juan). Often called Friday Island because of its dominant position in San Juan Island's Friday Harbor, the site was named by Wilkes after John G. Brown, mathematical instrument maker aboard the expedition's *Vincennes.*

Brownstown (Yakima). Originally called Bench due to its location on a plateau, it was renamed for businessman Reese Brown.

Brownsville (Kitsap). Named for original settler Solomon Brown.

Brush Prairie (Clark). Named by Elmorine Bowman after a brushy marsh on her father's homestead.

Bryant (Snohomish). Named for the Bryant Lumber and Shingle Co. that operated at the site in 1892.

Bryn Mawr, BRIN-MAHR (King). Platted in 1890 by William E. Parker and named by his wife after a town in their home state of Pennsylvania. It is a Welsh phrase meaning "big hill."

Buckley (Pierce). Site of Rainier State School for the mentally retarded, it was first known as Perkins Prairie after an early settler; was next called White River Siding; and in 1888 was given its present name to honor the superintendent of the Ellensburg-Tacoma division of the Northern Pacific Railroad.

Bucoda, byoo-KOH-duh (Thurston). Originally called Seatco, an Indian word meaning "devil," the town was the site of the first territorial prison, 1874–88. Prisoners worked adjacent coal mines owned by J. M. Buckley, Samuel Coulter, and John B. David. To avoid name confusion with Seattle, the three men coined a new name by using the first two initials of their surnames—Bu-Co-Da. The railroad adopted the name in 1874, the state in 1890.

Budd Inlet (Thurston). The southern extremity of Puget Sound on which Olympia is situated was named by Wilkes to honor Thomas A. Budd, who served as acting master of the expedition's *Peacock* and *Vincennes*. To the immediate west, two similar long and narrow inlets were named by Wilkes for expedition officers: Midshipmen Henry Eld and George M. Totten.

Buena, byoo-EN-uh (Yakima). Town bears the Spanish word for "good," but the pronunciation has been altered.

Burbank (Walla Walla). So named because it was the site of Burbank Power House operated by the Burbank Power and Water Co., which was named in honor of horticulturist Luther Burbank by Seattleite W. H. Parry.

Burien, BYOOR-eeuhn (King). The community takes its name from Lake Burien, which was incorrectly named for Gottlieb Burian [*sic*], who settled on the lakeshore in 1884.

Burley (Kitsap). Named for the creek that runs past the town, which, in turn, was named for an early settler.

Burlington (Skagit). Established as a logging camp in 1882, platted 1 January 1891, and named after Burlington, Vt.

Burnett (Pierce). Former coal-mining center derives its name from Charles M. Burnett, one of the Pacific Northwest's pioneer mine operators.

Burrows Island (Skagit). Named by Wilkes to honor naval hero Lt. William Burrows of the *Hornet*. He also named the waterway to the north as Hornets Harbor, but in the Spanish-English-American name reshuffling of the mid-1800s it was renamed Bellingham Channel. [*See* Allan Island.]

Burton (King). Situated on the east side of Vashon Island, the town was named in 1892 by Mrs. M. F. Hatch after her home town in Illinois.

Bush Point (Island). Named in 1855 by the U.S. Coast Survey because of "one or two clumps of trees and bushes."

Bush Prairie (Thurston). The prairie near Tumwater was named in honor of its first settler, George Bush, who came to the Puget Sound country with the Michael T. Simmons party in 1845 and was the first Negro to settle in what is now Washington State.

C

Calispell, KAL-is-pell (Pend Oreille). Lake, creek, railroad station, and former town derive their name (as did Kalispell, Mont.) from the word *kalispel,* meaning "camas root people," the Indian name for the tribe which French trappers called Pend d'Oreille because of their custom of wearing shell ear ornaments.

Camano Island, kuh-MAY-noh (Island). Wilkes named the island in honor of Master Commandant Thomas Macdonough, captain of the 26-gun *Saratoga* in its victory over the British on Lake Champlain during the War of 1812. Kellett dropped the name in 1847 in his effort to restore Spanish names, and bestowed the present title honoring Don Jacinto Caamano. However, Macdonough's ship's name remains in Saratoga Passage that separates Camano and Whidbey islands.

Camas, KAM-uhs (Clark). Originally called La Camas, the city takes its name from *Camassia esculenta,* a small bulb plant similar to the onion that was a favorite food of western Indians. The Nootka Indian word *chamass,* meaning "sweet fruit," was adopted into the Chinook jargon as *lacamass* and *camas.* Camas (just as Kamas, Ut., and Camas Valley, Ore.) was so named because it was a bountiful source of the blue-flowering Indian delicacy.

Camden (Pend Oreille). Named for J. N. Camden, United States Senator from West Virginia, who was a staunch supporter of the Great Northern Railroad during its western expansion.

Canby, Fort (Pacific). Completed in 1865 at Cape Disappointment, the post was named in 1874 by the War Department to honor Brev. Maj. Gen. Edward Richard Sprigg Canby of the U.S. Army, who, after distinguished service in the Mexican and Civil wars, was killed 11 April 1874 during the Modoc Indian War in California.

Capitol Lake (Thurston). Lake formed by damming Deschutes River estuary was named for its proximity to the state's Capitol Building in Olympia by the WSBGN in 1975.

Carbonado, kahr-buhn-AY-doh (Pierce). Situated on the Carbon River, the town derived its name from the stream which, in turn, was named after coal was discovered along its banks in the 1870s. It was a model community owned, planned, and operated by the Pacific Coast Coal Co., which installed paved streets and sewers and repainted the homes (average rent $14.00 a month). When the company ceased operation in the late 1920s, the pumps were removed, flooding five miles of collieries beyond reclamation.

Carbon River (Pierce). This tributary of the Puyallup River was called Upthascap River by Wilkes. With the discovery of coal along its banks in 1876 the river was renamed and the name extended to the Mt. Rainier glacier that is its source.

Carlsborg (Clallam). Founded and named by Carl J. Erickson during his construction of a branch line of the Chicago, Milwaukee and St. Paul Railroad in 1916.

Carlson (Lewis). Named for sawmill operator John Carlson, a Swedish immigrant, who was the first settler in the area.

Carlton (Okanogan). Named after early settler Carl Dillard.

Carnation (King). Renamed in 1917 by the state legislature to honor the nearby research farm operated by the Carnation Milk Products Co., developers of condensed milk. The town was originally called

Tolt, as it stands at the mouth of the Tolt River. [*See* Tolt River.]

Carr Inlet (Pierce). The waterway between Fox and McNeil islands was named by Wilkes for the expedition's Lt. Overton Carr.

Carrolls (Cowlitz). Name honors a Major Carroll, one of the area's first settlers.

Carson (Skamania). Originally called Ash because Lewis and Clark recorded sighting there the first ash trees on their western trek. The name was changed in 1895 when A. C. Tucker petitioned— with misread handwriting—for a post office to be named Casner after the first settler in the area.

Carter Point (Whatcom). William Carter, one of the Wilkes Expedition's petty officers, was the source of the name for the southern point of Lummi Island.

Cascade Mountains. In 1790 the Spaniard Manuel Quimper named the mountains Sierras Nevadas de S. Antonio; in 1792 Vancouver referred to the snowy range; in 1805 Lewis and Clark called them the western mountains; in his journal of 1823–27, botanist David Douglas wrote of the Cascade Range of mountains; and in 1841 Wilkes mapped them as the Cascade Range. The name appears to be a common usage, descriptive term that originated from the cascades in the Columbia River. Early travelers followed the course of the Columbia, utilizing the cascades as the best passage through the mountains. Immigrant records refer to "the mountains at the cascades." From 1834 to 1839 a nationwide, but futile, campaign was launched to change the name of the mountains to the President's Range and to call its greater peaks after former presidents. The Cascade Mountains are a continuation of the Sierra Nevada Mountains, extending north from California's Lassen Peak through Oregon and Washington to British Columbia, where the chain again changes name to Coast Mountains.

Case Inlet. The waterway in southern Puget Sound that forms the boundary between Mason and Pierce counties was named by Wilkes for the expedition's Lt. A. L. Case.

Casey, Fort (Island). Named for Brig. Gen. Thomas Lincoln Casey,

Chief of Engineers, U.S. Army, who died in 1896. Now a state park, the fort—along with Forts Flagler and Worden—was established in the late 1890s to guard Admiralty Inlet and prevent a hostile fleet from reaching Puget Sound.

Cashmere (Chelan). Originally known as Mission as a result of early Catholic missions established in the immediate vicinity by the Oblate Fathers in the 1850s and by the Jesuits in 1873. The town was renamed in 1903 to emulate in name, as well as fertility and valley setting, the beautiful and productive Vale of Kashmir in India.

Cashup (Whitman). Early community named for its first merchant and resort operator James H. Davis, who was widely known as Cash-up Davis because he extended no credit to anyone. The area is now incorporated into Steptoe Butte State Park.

Castle Island (San Juan). Situated just off the southern tip of Lopez Island, this formidable appearing island was first named in the U.S. Coast Survey chart of 1855 as Old Hundred Island. It was given its present descriptive name on the British Admiralty chart of 1858–60.

Castle Rock (Cowlitz). Because of its castle-like appearance, homesteader William Huntington in 1853 so named a 150-foot-high, one-acre-square rock on his donation claim. When a town developed on the site, it adopted the general usage name.

Cathcart (Snohomish). Named in honor of Isaac Cathcart, a prominent lumberman who settled there in the community's early days.

Cathlamet, KATH-LA-muht (Wahkiakum). This county seat on the Columbia River derived its name from the Kathlamet Indians. The tribal name was derived from the Chinook word *calamet,* meaning "stone," and was given to the tribe because they lived along a stretch of rocky river bed. [*See* Wahkiakum County.]

Cattle Point (San Juan). The southeastern tip of San Juan Island was used by Hudson's Bay Co. as a loading and unloading point for cattle prior to the boundary dispute of 1858.

Cedar Falls (King). Descriptive of the community's location near the falls on the Cedar River, a portion of which serves as the Seattle watershed.

Cedar Grove (King). Derives its name from a stand of lowland cedar and its juxtaposition to Cedar Mountain.

Cedarhome (Snohomish). Settled in 1870 by Swedish immigrants who built their homes in a cedar forest and named the town for its setting.

Cedonia, SEE-doh-neeuh (Stevens). Initially called Cadonia by early settlers and modified with establishment of the post office in 1898, the name is an adaptation of that of the Persian tribes referred to in the Old Testament.

Centerville (Klickitat). So named because of its mid-valley location.

Centralia (Lewis). The city was founded by George Washington, mulatto son of a Virginia slave and a white serving girl. Washington settled at the townsite in 1852 and platted it as Centerville in 1875. Because of confusion of names with Centerville in Klickitat County, a public meeting accepted the recommendation of a former resident of Centralia, Ill., who suggested the name of his home town as being reminiscent of—but more distinctive than—Centerville.

Central Park (Grays Harbor). So named because of its location between Aberdeen and Montesano.

Ceres, SEER-eez (Lewis). The farming community was named for the ancient Roman goddess of agriculture.

Chatham, Mt., CHATH-uhm (Jefferson). Visible from Port Discovery Bay, which was named by Vancouver for his ship *Discovery,* the peak was named by the U.S. Coast Survey after Vancouver's armed tender *Chatham.*

Chattaroy, CHAT-er-oi (Spokane). No official version of the definition of the name exists in the community. It was changed *circa* 1890 by pressure of Mrs. D. C. Cowgill, wife of the first postmaster, from its original name of Kidd—which she felt was inappropriate. However, historical records credit her with different explanations of the name source—river named in a poem she read; adaptation of *chateau roi* (French, meaning "royal palace"); restoration of the original Indian name for the site.

Chehalis, chuh-HAY-lis (Lewis). City on the Chehalis River was established on the donation claim of S. S. Saunders in 1851 as Saunders Bottom; in 1858 a post office opened under the name Saundersville, and in 1870 the post office was given its present name. The state legislature officially recognized the name change on 5 November 1879 and designated the town as county seat in 1883.

Chehalis River. The river that drains the southern Olympic Mountains rises in Pacific and Cowlitz counties and flows through Lewis, Thurston, and Grays Harbor counties to enter Grays Harbor at Aberdeen. The Indian word *chehalis,* meaning "shining sands," was originally the name of a native village at the river's mouth, but settlers used it for the river and the Indian tribe living along its banks. The name has been widely applied to geographic features in the region: Chehalis Creek and Chehalis Point in Grays Harbor County and the Chehalis Indian Reservation in Thurston County. There once was a Chehalis City in Grays Harbor County, which, itself, was known as Chehalis County until 1915.

Chelan, she-LAN (Chelan). City and adjacent geographic points—river, falls, butte, mountains—named for Lake Chelan, which the Indians appropriately called Tsill-ane or "deep water." The 55-mile-long lake is 1,500 feet deep, which places its bottom 400 feet below sea level. The city of Chelan was established as Fort Chelan in 1879 by the U.S. Army, which laid out the government townsite with streets 100 feet wide. Chelan Falls, now a railroad station town located where the four-mile-long Chelan River joins the Columbia River, was originally a steamboat landing.

Chelan County; 2,931 sq. mi.; 3rd in size; seat: Wenatchee. Established 13 March 1899.

Cheney (Spokane). Depot Springs lost out to Spokane Falls as the seat of Spokane County so residents shifted their goal from government to higher education. They renamed the city for Benjamin P. Cheney, one of the founders of the Great Northern Railroad, and solicited his support for an academy. He responded with $10,000, and the resultant school, Cheney Academy, became one of the state's first normal schools and eventually Eastern Washington State College. [*See* Spokane County.]

Chenois Creek, chen-OOS (Grays Harbor). The community is situated at the site of a former Indian village of the same name. The meaning of the word is unknown.

Chenowith, CHEN-o-with (Skamania). Named for attorney F. A. Chenowith, an early homesteader in the area, who as a member of the Oregon Territorial Legislature lobbied for creation of Washington Territory.

Chesaw, CHEE-saw (Okanogan). Named for a Chinese miner, Chee Saw, who married an Indian and remained in the area as a farmer after the placer workings were exhausted in the 1860s.

Chetlo Harbor, CHET-loh (Pacific). The name is an Indian word meaning "oyster."

Chewelah, chuh-WEE-luh (Stevens). The town adopted the original Indian name for the mouth of the creek at which it is situated: *chawelah,* meaning "small, striped snake."

Chico, CHEE-koh (Kitsap). Named in 1889 to honor Indian chief Chico, who lived in the area.

Chief Joseph Dam (Douglas). Named for Chief Joseph of the Nez Perce, who led his tribe's 1,000-mile battle against the U.S. Army while attempting to escape from Oregon to Canada. Following capture in 1877, the chief was confined to the Colville Indian Reservation, and at his death in 1904 was buried at Nespelem in Okanogan County.

Chillowist, CHIL-uh-wist (Okanogan). Railway station, creek, canyon, and early trail to the Methow Valley all named for Indian Charley Chiliwist, who lived at the mouth of the creek.

Chimacum, CHI-muh-kuhm (Jefferson). Both the creek and town on its banks were named after the Chimakum Indians, a small but warlike tribe that lived between Port Townsend and Hood Canal.

Chinook, shi-NOOK (Pacific). Named for the Tsinuk Indian tribes that occupied the lower banks of the Columbia River. Their strategic position established them as traders with inland and coastal tribes prior to the arrival of the white man, and thus their language, augmented by French and English, became the Chinook jargon used by early traders and pioneers. As a result the word *chinook* is frequently used in the Pacific Northwest as a term for innumerable geographic points, for a warm snow-melting wind, for extra large King salmon, etc.

Chopaka, chu-PAK-uh (Okanogan). Mountain and nearby railroad station bear as their name the Indian word meaning "high mountain."

Chuckanut, CHUHK-uh-nut (Whatcom). A suburb of Bellingham, a bay, an island, and a rock at the southwest corner of the Whatcom County mainland carry an Indian name of unknown definition. The bay was called Puerto del Socorro or "Port of Help" by Eliza.

Cinebar, SI-ne-bahr (Lewis). A corruption of the word *cinnabar,* a bright red mercury ore, after several such mines that once existed in the area.

Clallam County, KLAL-uhm; 1,753 sq. mi.; 20th in size; seat: Port Angeles. County, river, bay, and community of Clallam Bay, as well as other geographic points, derive their names from that of the Indian tribe that inhabited the area. There are various recorded phonetic versions of the Indian word, generally accepted to mean "brave people": *s'kallam, challam, callam.* The tribe's name for themselves was Nu-sklaim or "strong people," while their Makah neighbors called them "the clam people" from *klo-lub,* "clam," and *aht,* "man." Even the Territorial Law of 26 April 1854, which officially created the county, initiated a different, but short-lived spelling—Clalm.

Claquato, KLA-kwa-toh (Lewis). Platted *circa* 1852 by Louis H. Davis, operator of both a gristmill and a sawmill, who gave the town the Indian name meaning "high land."

Clark County; 633 sq. mi.; 34th in size; seat: Vancouver. Named in honor of Capt. William Clark of the Lewis and Clark Expedition. Correctly spelled by the Oregon Territorial Legislature, the name was corrupted with an "e" at the end in the first legislative journal of the newly formed Washington Territory in 1854. The error persisted in official documents, in newspapers and books, and on maps until corrected to its present and proper spelling by the state legislature in its 1925 extraordinary session. [*See* Lewis County.]

Clark Island (San Juan). Clark and nearby Barnes Island were named by Wilkes to honor naval heroes of the War of 1812. Clark Island is the namesake of Midshipman John Clark, who was killed during Adm. Oliver Perry's battle of Lake Erie. Both islands were originally named by the Spanish in 1791 as Islas de Aquays, a portion of the long name of the viceroy of Mexico who Eliza so often honored in his place naming.

Clarkston (Asotin). The travels of Capts. William Clark and Meriwether Lewis down the Snake River are commemorated by cities on opposing banks: Clarkston, Wash., and Lewiston, Ida.

Clayton (Stevens). Established in 1889 and named for the commercially valuable deposits of clay in the area.

Clearlake (Skagit). Platted in 1890 as Mountain View and subsequently renamed for a nearby lake.

Clearview (Snohomish). The name is descriptive of its panoramic setting.

Clearwater (Jefferson). So named for the sparkling water of the stream at the community's site.

Cle Elum, klee-EL-uhm (Kittitas). River and town bear the Indian name meaning "swift water." The triple wide streets are due to the nagging of Barbara Steiner Reed, wife of the town's founder, who expected the coal-mining center to become the Pittsburgh of the West and wanted it to surpass its eastern counterpart in beauty.

Clinton (Island). The Whidbey Island community was originally a steamboat refueling stop named after woodcutter John G. Phinney, but in 1892 the growing town was renamed for Clinton, Mich.

Clipper (Whatcom). Named in 1900 after the Clipper Shingle Co.

Clyde Hill (King). Name coined by the first mayor as descriptive of the town's location on a hill bisected by 92nd Ave. NE, which was known as Clyde Road until World War II. The road name was originally suggested by a Scotsman, who found the area reminiscent of the topography of the Firth of Clyde in his homeland.

Cohasset, koh-HA-suht (Grays Harbor). Named in 1892 by Aberdeen banker John Wooding for the resort town of Cohassett, Mass. A railroad station in Kittitas County is also named for the same source.

Colbert (Spokane). Established as a sawmill town called Drygoon in 1890, it was renamed in 1902 for Harry Colbert, storekeeper and postmaster.

Colby (Kitsap). In the mid-1880s, lumps of coal were discovered along a small stream, giving rise to the name of Coal Bay, which was later shortened to Colby. The nearby community of South Colby was so named because of its position on the opposite shore of Yukon Harbor.

Colchester (Kitsap). The community is located between Colby and Manchester, and its name is a coined composite of the two names.

Colfax (Whitman). The county seat townsite was settled in 1870 as Belleville and renamed to honor Vice President Schuyler Colfax during U. S. Grant's term as President.

College Place (Walla Walla). Named in 1882 for the community that grew up around the Seventh Day Adventist Church's Walla Walla College.

Colton (Whitman). Town name combines the first and last three letters, respectively, of the names of two early settlers—Cole and Worthington.

Columbia County; 860 sq. mi.; 31st in size; seat: Dayton. Named in honor of the Columbia River when the county was formed on 11 November 1895. The original name suggested, but vetoed by Territorial Governor Elisha P. Ferry, was Ping, in homage to Territorial Councilman Elisha Ping.

Columbia River. Discovered by American Capt. Robert Gray and named for his ship *Columbia Rediviva* on 11 May 1792. Second only to the Missouri-Mississippi in annual volume, the river rises in Columbia Lake, B.C., Canada, and flows 1,270 miles—700 in Washington State—to the Pacific Ocean. It forms three-quarters of the Washington-Oregon boundary. [*See* Grays Harbor.]

Colville, KAWL-vil (Stevens). Established by the Hudson's Bay Co. as Fort Colvile in 1825 and named for Andrew Colvile, London governor of the fur-trading company. A few miles east, the U.S. Army established a post under Maj. Pinkney Lougenbeel, and in his honor the place was known as Pinkney City. When the county was organized in 1863 Pinkney was renamed Colville and designated as the county seat.

Colville Island, KOHL-vil (San Juan). Though the pronunciation differs slightly from that of the city, both Colville Island and Point Colville at the southeastern tip of Lopez Island were named for Andrew Colvile, governor of the Hudson's Bay Co., 1852–56.

Colvos Passage, KOHL-vohs. Waterway between Vashon Island and the mainland that forms the boundary between King and Kitsap counties was named by Wilkes for the expedition's George W. Colvocoressis. Wilkes considered the midshipman's surname to be too long for geographic honors, so he shortened it for the official charts.

Colvos Rocks (Jefferson). The rocks at the entrance to Port Ludlow Harbor were named for a midshipman in the Wilkes Expedition.

Commencement Bay (Pierce). So named by Wilkes as it was the starting point, on 15 May 1841, for the expedition's hydrographic survey of southern Puget Sound under Lt. Cadwalader Ringgold in the brig *Porpoise*.

Conconully, kahn-kuh-NEL-ee (Okanogan). Indian name for the valley surrounding the townsite was Conconulp, meaning "money hole," because it abounded with beaver, whose skins were as good as cash at Fort Okanogan.

Concrete (Skagit). Founded in 1890 by Magnus Miller as Baker after the nearby tributary of the Skagit River. In 1905, the main industry switched from a lumber mill to a lime quarry. With establishment of a Portland Cement Co. plant, the community was renamed Cement City, and was subsequently given its present title.

Connell, kah-NEL (Franklin). Named for an employee of the Northern Pacific Railroad.

Constance, Mt. (Jefferson). Named by Capt. George Davidson of the U.S. Coast Survey in 1856 for a member of the Fauntleroy family. [*See* Fauntleroy Cove.]

Constitution, Mt. (San Juan). Named for the famous United States frigate *Constitution,* it is one of the few remaining vestiges of Wilkes's attempt to rename the San Juan Islands the Navy Archipelago. [*See* Orcas Island.]

Conway (Skagit). The Skagit River townsite was settled by Thomas P. Jones and Charles Villenueve in 1873. After arrival of the Great Northern Railroad in 1891, Jones officially platted the town and named it for his former home in Wales.

Cook (Skamania). Originally a steamboat landing on the Columbia River, the town was named in 1908 for Charles A. Cook, who homesteaded the townsite.

Copalis Beach, koh-PAY-lis (Grays Harbor). The ocean resort town, situated at the mouth of Copalis Creek, was named for the Indian tribe, called Chepalis by Lewis and Clark, that inhabited the area. Repetition of the name is found directly inland at Copalis Crossing, a railroad station community near the Humptulips River.

Corfu, KOR-foo (Grant). Named for one of the Ionian Islands west of Greece by H. R. Williams.

Cormorant Passage, KOR-moor-ant (Pierce). Waterway east of Ketron Island was named in 1846 by British Admiralty chartographer R. M. Inskip to honor the paddle sloop, H.M.S. *Cormorant,* the first naval steam vessel in Puget Sound waters.

Cornet, kor-NET (Island). Community and bay on northern Whidbey Island bear the name of John Cornet, who settled there with his Indian wife in the 1860s.

Cosmopolis, kahz-MAH-poh-lis (Grays Harbor). Named in 1853 by R. Brunn, a French homesteader who utilized the Greek language to coin the title, "city of the whole world."

Cottonwood Island (Cowlitz). Situated in the Columbia River near the mouth of the Cowlitz River, it was initially known by the Indian name Kanem, meaning "canoe," but was renamed because of its stand of trees.

Cougar (Cowlitz). Residents submitted several wild animal names to postal authorities, and this one was selected.

Coulee City, KOO-lee (Grant). So named because of its location in Grand Coulee, the dry course of the Columbia River in earlier ages.

Coulee Dam (Okanogan). So named because of its location at the site of Grand Coulee Dam. The city is physically situated in three counties—Okanogan, Grant, and Douglas—and incorporation required a special enactment by the state legislature.

Coupeville (Island). Whidbey Island's Penn Cove was settled by Col. Isaac Ebey in 1850; two years later retired sea captain Thomas Coupe homesteaded nearby. Ebey was beheaded by raiding Haida Indians in 1857, while Coupe had the county seat platted and named for him. [*See* Fort Ebey.]

Cove (King). Descriptive of its location on small Vashon Island Bay.

Coweman River, kow-EE-muhn. This tributary of the Cowlitz River was initially called Gobar's River after the Hudson's Bay Co. herder Anton Gobar, who pastured stock near the present townsite of Kelso. It was changed to a derivative of the Cowlitz word *ko-wee-na*, meaning "short man"—the native title of the river in recognition of a dwarf-sized Indian who lived on the river bank.

Cowiche, kow-ICH-ee (Yakima). An adaptation of the Indian word *kwiwichess*, meaning "foot log," in reference to a bridge over the nearby creek.

Cowlitz Bay, KOW-litz (San Juan). Situated on the southwestern shore of Waldron Island, the bay is so far removed from the southwestern Washington area inhabited by the Cowlitz Indians that it is assumed that it was named after the Hudson's Bay Co. vessel, *Cowlitz*.

Cowlitz County; 1,146 sq. mi.; 25th in size; seat: Kelso. Derived from the Indian *tawallitch* and spelled 16 different ways in early records (Coweliske, Cowelits, and Kaoulis being the most common), the word "Cowlitz" was applied to both the river and the Salish tribe that wandered its banks. Its exact definition is lost in antiquity, but it means roughly "capturing the medicine spirit," from the tribe's custom of utilizing one specific prairie along the river as a site for young braves to commune in isolation with the Great Spirit. In addition to its adoption as a county name in 1854, the word has been affixed to a dozen geographic entities, including a glacier and a pass near the river's source.

Crater (Grant). Railway station so named because the tracks border an extinct volcanic crater.

Creosote (Kitsap). Established as Eagle Harbor in 1884 and changed to its present name with the establishment of a post office in 1908 to tie in to a creosoting plant that was the community's main industry.

Crescent, Lake (Clallam). Name is descriptive of the shape of the lake, which is more than 600 feet deep.

Creston (Lincoln). So named because it is the railroad station situated at the crest, or highest point, along the railroad tracks in the Big Bend country.

Crewport (Yakima). Established as a transient labor camp and so named because of the farm crews that resided there while working the various crops of the valley.

Crocker (Pierce). Named for a California capitalist who was an investor in the Northern Pacific Railroad, which made the site a station stop.

Cromwell (Pierce). Named for J. B. Cromwell, former Tacoma postmaster, who established a summer residence on Wollochet Bay at the southern extremity of Kitsap Peninsula, *circa* 1902.

Cultus Bay, KUL-tis (Island). Extremely shallow bay at the southern end of Whidbey Island bears the Chinook jargon word meaning "bad" or "worthless." [*See* Useless Bay.]

Cumberland (King). Coal-mining town named in 1893 for the famous Pennsylvania coal region.

Cunningham (Adams). First established as a railroad station named Scott, the present community was platted in 1901 by land promoter and preacher W. R. Cunningham.

Curlew, KER-loo (Ferry). Town on a creek that drains a lake, all of which carry the English version of the Indian word *karanips,* for the "curlew," a snipe-like bird once prevalent in the region.

Curtis (Lewis). Named for the first postmaster.

Cushman, Lake (Mason). Named in honor of Orrington Cushman, packer and interpreter for Gov. Isaac I. Stevens during the treaty negotiations with Puget Sound Indians in 1854. Known as "Devil Cush," the frontiersman advocated putting all western Washington Indians on one giant reservation on the western shore of Hood Canal.

Cusick, KYOO-sik (Pend Oreille). Named for Joe Cusick, early homesteader in the area.

Custer (Whatcom). Named in 1886 in honor of Albert W. Custer, early settler and first storekeeper and postmaster.

Cypress Island (Skagit). Erroneously named in 1792 by Vancouver because he misidentified the native junipers as cypress trees. Eliza's chart of 1791 lists the island as Isla de S. Vincente, another instance in which he bestowed a segment of his sponsor's name on a geographic feature.

d

Dabop Bay, DAY-bahp (Jefferson). Although spelled "Dabob" on some recent maps, the large bay on the west shore of Hood Canal was charted by Wilkes as Dabop, an Indian word of unknown meaning.

Dahlia (Wahkiakum). When the post office application was filed in 1910, the first postmaster-to-be Grant Elliott switched the boat landing's name from Elliott Point to Dahlia to avoid confusion with Point Elliot near Mukilteo. Thus, the primarily Scandinavian populated settlement—for unrecorded reasons—came to bear the name of a flower native to Latin America, but named for Swedish botanist Anders Dahl.

Daisy (Stevens). Named for one of two nearby silver-lead mines, the Tempest and the Daisy.

Dalkena, dahl-KEN-uh (Pend Oreille). Name is a composite of Dalton and Kennedy, early lumber-mill owners in the town.

Dallesport, DALZ-port (Klickitat). The county seat until 1878, the Columbia River town was successively known as Rockport, Grand Dalles, and North Dalles, and finally in 1937 was given its present name. All titles attempted to identify it as the Washington shore counterpart of The Dalles, Ore. [*See* The Dalles Dam.]

Danas Passage, DAN-nas. Waterway between Thurston and Mason

35

counties was named Dana's Passage by Wilkes for the expedition's geologist, James Dwight Dana.

Danville (Ferry). The town was named for a merchant who built his store straddling the United States–Canadian border. Customs officers, suspicious that he was selling items bought in one country to customers of the other country without payment of duty, forced removal of the business to a spot south of the border.

Darrington (Snohomish). Intended to honor an early resident named Barrington, but the first letter was misread on the post office application.

Dartford (Spokane). Named for early settler Herbert W. Dart, who established the community's first gristmill, sawmill, and post office.

Dash Point (Pierce). Name source unverified. Various versions exist, including reference to use of the promontory as a geodetic survey point on early maps.

Davenport (Lincoln). County seat was named for J. C. Davenport, first storekeeper.

Davidson Rock (San Juan). Large rock southeast of Lopez Island honors Capt. George Davidson of the U.S. Coast Survey, who extensively explored and charted Puget Sound waters in the late 1850s.

Day Island (Pierce). Island west of Tacoma was named by Wilkes to honor Stephen E. Days, one of the expedition's hospital stewards.

Dayton (Columbia). The county seat was platted by and named for Jesse N. Day, a former West Virginian who came to the Oregon Territory in 1848.

Deadman Bay (San Juan). This small bay on the western coast of San Juan Island is reputed to be the grave site of the first white man to die on the island—a laborer killed by a cook.

Deadman Creek (Garfield). In the blizzard winter of 1861–62, two miners en route to Idaho's Orofino gold fields froze to death. In the spring their bodies were found at the place now known as Deadman Hollow, through which the stream flows. A village named Deadman was abandoned in 1880.

Decatur Island, di-KAY-ter (San Juan). Named by Wilkes in honor of Stephen Decatur, one of the most famous United States naval officers. In 1804 with a volunteer crew, he slipped into Tripoli Harbor and burned the United States frigate *Philadelphia* (commanded by William Bainbridge) that had been captured by the Barbary Pirates—a feat described by British admiral Lord Nelson as "the most daring of the age." In the War of 1812 he commanded the *United States* in victory over the British ship *Macedonian* and captained the *President* in defeat of the *Endymion*. In 1815 Decatur returned to the Mediterranean in command of the fleet that forced peace on the Barbary States of North Africa. He was the originator of the patriotic aphorism, "Our country, right or wrong." At age 40, Decatur was shot to death in a duel with Capt. James Barron, another naval officer. His second in the duel was Commodore William Bainbridge. [*See* Bainbridge Island.]

Decatur Reef (Kitsap). Southeast of Bainbridge Island, the reef by odd coincidence ties together the names of two naval officers who were close personal friends and heroes of the War of 1812: William Bainbridge and Stephen Decatur. Wilkes named the island for Bainbridge; the reef honors Decatur only indirectly. During the Indian War of 1855–56 Seattle was defended by a sloop-of-war named for the nemesis of the Barbary Pirates. Following the battle of Seattle, the *Decatur* ran aground on the reef which was then given the vessel's name. [*See* James Island in San Juan County.]

Deception Island (Island). Small island at the western border of Island and Skagit counties was named in 1854 by the U.S. Coast Survey after nearby Deception Pass.

Deception Pass. The channel separating Whidbey and Fidalgo islands was named by Vancouver because it had deceptively appeared to be a narrow bay rather than a passageway. [*See* Whidbey Island.]

Deepcreek (Spokane). Originally named Deep Creek Falls as descriptive of its location, the name was shortened to its present form in 1894.

Deep River (Wahkiakum). Small village situated on a slough the Indians called *alimicut,* meaning "deep river."

Deer Harbor (San Juan). Small village and harbor—complete with a Fawn Island—on the southwestern shore of Orcas Island were so named because of the large deer population on Orcas.

Deer Park (Spokane). Name recalls the hunting excellence of the area in pioneer days.

Defiance, Point (Pierce). Now the city of Tacoma's major park, the point was named by Wilkes, who felt that if properly fortified it "would bid defiance to any attack."

Deming (Whatcom). Named for the Deming Land Co., which platted the townsite. First postmistress in 1888 was Mrs. S. J. Deming, who was no relation to Frank and George Deming of the development company.

Denison (Spokane). Originally named Buckeye for the Buckeye Lumber Co. When the firm moved away, the town was renamed Pratt, and then was given its present name by F. H. Buell for his wife's maiden name.

Deschutes River, duh-SHOOTS (Thurston). The French term meaning falls was given to the river by Hudson's Bay traders. The falls, the site of the first permanent American settlement north of the Columbia River, are now known as Tumwater Falls. [*See* Tumwater.]

Des Moines, duh-MOINZ (King). Settled in 1870 and named in 1889 for the Des Moines Improvement Co., which, in turn, had been named by one of its principals for his home town in Iowa. In the 17th century, French explorers Louis Jolliet and Jacques Marquette named a midwestern river Riviere de Moingouens for a tribe of Indians. In time the tribal name was shortened to de Moings, which was eventually misinterpreted as the French *de moines,* meaning "of the monks."

Destruction Island (Jefferson). On 14 July 1775 Spanish Capt. Juan Francisco de la Bodega y Quadra anchored the *Sonora* at a small island offshore from the Hoh River and sent seven men for wood and water. After Indians killed the crew, Bodega y Quadra named the island Isla de Dolores, meaning "Island of Sorrows." In 1887 English Capt. Charles W. Barclay in the *Imperial Eagle* sent a crew ashore to explore the Hoh River, and all six were killed by Indians, so he named the stream Destruction River. In time the river was officially named the Hoh, after the Indian band living at its mouth, and the term Destruction was affixed to the island. [*See* Hoh River.]

Dewatto, de-WAH-toh (Mason). The Hood Canal community bears an adaptation of the Indian place name *du-a-to,* meaning "home of evil spirits who make men crazy." In Indian legend, spirits, called *tub-ta-ba,* emerged from the bowels of the earth in the Dewatto Bay area and attempted to enter the bodies of normal warriors.

Dewey (Skagit). The Fidalgo Island community honors Adm. George Dewey, victor at the battle of Manila Bay in the Spanish-American War.

Diablo, dee-AHB-loh (Whatcom). Dam, reservoir, and company town operated by Seattle City Light take their name from narrow Diablo Canyon on the Skagit River. The word is Spanish for "devil" and was assigned by a prospector in the 1880s. The rugged area also possesses a Big Devil Mountain, a Little Devil Mountain, and a sharp bend in the river called Devil's Elbow. [*See* Newhalem.]

Diamond Lake (Pend Oreille). Summer resort community that bears the name of the adjacent lake, which was purportedly named in 1888 by hunters who found a single playing card—the ace of diamonds—on the lake shore.

Dieringer, DAIR-in-jer (Pierce). Named for Tacoma restaurateur Joseph C. Dieringer, who speculated in land in the area.

Dinner Island (San Juan). In Griffin Bay on the southeastern coast of San Juan Island, the island was so named because a landing party from a British vessel ate there.

Disappointment, Cape (Pacific). On 17 August 1775 Spanish explorer Bruno Heceta found a bay he believed to be river-fed. On 6 July 1788 English explorer John Meares failed to find the assumed river marked on Spanish charts, so he changed the name of the bay from Ensenada de Heceta to Deception Bay and that of the north cape from San Rogue to Cape Disappointment. Four years later the river was discovered by American Capt. Robert Gray. [*See* Columbia River.]

Discovery Bay (Jefferson). Community name is a tie in to the bay which bears the name of Vancouver's ship. [*See* Port Discovery Bay.]

Dishman (Spokane). Named for A. T. Dishman, who founded the town in 1889 and established its first industry—a granite quarry.

Disney, Point (San Juan). The southern tip of Waldron Island was named by Wilkes for Solomon Disney, one of the expedition's sailmaker's mates.

Dixie (Walla Walla). The first settler was Herman C. Actor, but he was overshadowed by the Kershaw brothers, a musical trio who would entertain any visitor with their favorite tune, "Dixie." They became known as the Dixie Boys and their homestead as Dixie Crossing.

Dockton (King). A town on Maury Island named by the Puget Sound Dry Dock Co., which had an operation there.

Doebay (San Juan). The proliferation of deer on Orcas Island accounts for the name of the community, as well as a bevy of geographic points, such as Doe Bay, Doe Island, Deer Point, and Buck Bay.

Dosewallips River, dohs-ee-WAH-lips (Jefferson). The name derives from Dos-wail-opsh, the name of a legendary man in the Twana Indian mythology who was turned into a mountain that is the river's source.

Dot Island (Skagit). Three small islands east of Guemes Island in Padilla Bay were charted by Wilkes as Porpoise Rocks after the expedition's brig *Porpoise*. The U.S. Coast and Geodetic Survey individualized the names to Saddlebag, Huckleberry, and Dot islands in 1904.

Doty (Lewis). Named for C. A. Doty, who established a sawmill there in 1900.

Double Bluff (Island). The name of the western cape of Useless Bay is descriptive of its appearance.

Doughty, Point, DOW-tee (San Juan). This point on the western coast of Orcas Island was named by Wilkes for John Doughty, a petty officer aboard the expedition's *Peacock*.

Douglas (Douglas). Named in 1884 by Ole Rudd in honor of the county in which it is located.

Douglas County; 1,841 sq. mi.; 17th in size; seat: Waterville. Named 28 April 1883 in honor of Stephen A. Douglas, U.S. Senator from Illinois and arch political rival of Abraham Lincoln. [*See* Lincoln County.] A railroad station community in the western portion of the county was given the same name as a geographic tie in to the county. However, Douglas Mountain in adjacent Okanogan County was named after Douglas Joe, an early prospector.

Drayton Passage (Pierce). Both the waterway west of Anderson Island and the harbor in northwestern Whatcom County were named by Wilkes to honor the expedition's artist, John Drayton. [*See* Semiahmoo Bay.]

Dryad (Lewis). Named by the Northern Pacific Railroad in 1890. The name means "nymph of the woods."

Dryden (Chelan). Named in 1907 for a Canadian horticulturist who toured the area as a guest of James J. Hill, president of the Great Northern Railway.

Dry Falls (Grant). During the prehistoric period of glaciation, an ice dam at the present site of Coulee Dam diverted the Columbia River along the present path of the Grand Coulee. The falls thus created, many times higher than Niagara, were left dry when the glaciers melted and the river resumed its former course. The area is the site of Dry Falls State Park.

Duckabush River, DUHK-uh-b<u>oo</u>sh (Jefferson). The river flows into Hood Canal near a small community with the same name, which is derived from the Indian word *do-hi-a-boos,* meaning "reddish face," for the appearance of mountain bluffs in the region.

Dungeness, DUHN-gen-es (Clallam). In 1792 Vancouver wrote, "The low sandy point of land, which from its great resemblance to Dungeness in the British Channel, I called New Dungeness." The name Dungeness has been extended from spit to harbor, river, and town.

Du Pont (Pierce). Named for the powder plant of E. I. du Pont de Nemours Powder Co. at the site, the company-built community occupies the area where once stood old Fort Nisqually, a Hudson's Bay Co. trading post established in 1833. [*See* Nisqually.]

Dusty (Whitman). Purportedly so named by early residents because it was.

Duvall, doo-VAWL (King). Named for James Duvall, who homesteaded the Cherry Valley land in 1875 on which the town was platted in 1910 by John D. Bird.

Duwamish River, doo-WAH-mish (King). Name derived from Indian word *dewampsh,* meaning "the people living on the river."

Dye Inlet (Kitsap). Named by Wilkes for the expedition's assistant taxidermist, W. W. Dyes.

Eagledale (Kitsap). Community name ties in to its location on the south shore of Eagle Harbor, which was named by Wilkes. Presumably the expedition felt the harbor's outline to be reminiscent of an eagle's shape. Theory is enforced by his naming the bay's north and south capes Wing Point and Bill Point.

Easton (Kittitas). Named for its location near the eastern entrance to the Northern Pacific Railroad tunnel through the Cascade Mountains. At the opposite end there was once a railroad station community named Weston.

Eastsound (San Juan). Community was named for its location on the large bay, East Sound, on the east side of Orcas Island. On the opposite side of the island is another bay called West Sound, indicating the origin of the harbors' names.

Eatonville (Pierce). Named after T. C. Van Eaton, who platted the townsite in 1880.

Ebey, Fort (Island). The state park near Point Partridge, midway on the west shore of Whidbey Island, and Ebey Slough, a tidal stream that drains into the Snohomish River north of Everett, commemorate one of the great early pioneers, Col. Isaac Ebey. A man of culture and education, he named Olympia, served as government customs collector, first settled the Coupeville area, and in 1850 founded Ebey's Landing, a once-thriving stop for Puget Sound commerce opposite Port Townsend. However, rather than his personal contributions to the territory's development, he is most remembered for his tragic death. On the night of 11 August 1857, Haida Indians from British Columbia, seeking face-saving revenge for earlier defeat by the cannons of the U.S.S. *Massachusetts,* raided Whidbey Island. They preselected Ebey as their victim. They awakened him at his farmhouse, shot and decapitated him, and fled back to the Queen Charlotte Islands with his head. Several years later the grisly trophy was recovered by the Hudson's Bay Co. and returned for burial with his body.

Ebey's Prairie (Island). Site of the donation homestead filed by Col. Isaac Ebey, early Whidbey Island settler who was murdered by marauding British Columbia Indians.

Edgewood (Pierce). Named for an early settler.

Edison (Skagit). Town on Samish Bay named in 1876 after inventor Thomas Alva Edison.

Ediz Hook, EE-diz (Clallam). A three-mile-long sand spit that forms Port Angeles Harbor was named by Kellett in 1847 from the Indian word *yennis,* meaning "good place." For a short period it was called False Dungeness for its similarity to the more easterly Dungeness Harbor. [*See* Port Angeles.]

Edmonds (Snohomish). The name is an error in spelling, but not in pronunciation. It was named in honor of Vermont's famous senator, George F. Edmunds, by an admirer who served the city as first postmaster.

Edwall (Lincoln). Named for pioneer Peter Edwall, who platted the townsite.

Eglon, EG-luhn (Kitsap). Small beach community's name is a postal official's misreading of the name of Egdon, one of the kings in the Old Testament.

Elbe, EL-bee (Pierce). Name honors the Elbe Valley in Germany, old-country home of early settler Henry C. Lutkens.

Elberton (Whitman). Community was founded at the time of Elbert Wait's death and named for him at his father's request. Once site of the world's largest prune dryer, the residents—a total of 20 voters—voted to disincorporate the town in 1966.

Eld Inlet (Thurston). One of the southern arms of Puget Sound named by Wilkes to honor an officer of the expedition. [*See* Budd Inlet.]

Electric City (Grant). Born during construction of Grand Coulee Dam, the town was so named because of its proximity to a major source of electrical power. Planners also hoped to make it a model all-electric—cooking and heating—community. The 1934 name stuck, the all-electric concept did not.

Electron (Pierce). Community's name derived from its location at the site of an electric power plant on the Puyallup River.

Elgin (Pierce). Initially called Minter after the first postmaster, the community was renamed in 1893 for Elgin, Ill.

Eliza Island, el-EE-za (Whatcom). The small island in Bellingham Bay was named by Wilkes in honor of Spanish Navy Lt. Francisco Eliza, who explored the region in 1791.

Elk (Spokane). Name chosen by early settler Mrs. David R. Mace because of the elk herds that once browsed in the area.

Ellensburg (Kittitas). In 1875 John A. Shoudy platted and named the county seat town for his wife—Mary Ellen Stewart Shoudy.

Ellinor, Mt. (Jefferson). Named by Capt. George Davidson of the U.S. Coast Survey in 1856 for a member of the Fauntleroy family. [*See* Fauntleroy Cove.]

Elliot Point (Snohomish). Named Point Elliott by Wilkes, presumably to honor one of three men in the expedition with similar surnames. On 22 January 1855 Governor Isaac I. Stevens selected "Muckl-te-oh or Point Elliott" as site for a treaty parley in which the Indians ceded to the United States the coastal lands from Seattle to the Canadian border. [*See* Elliott Bay; Mukilteo.]

Elliott Bay (King). Seattle's harbor was named by Wilkes. There were three men on the expedition roster with similar names: the Reverend J. L. Elliott, Midshipman Samuel Elliott, and 1st Class Boy George Elliot. It was initially believed that the bay was named for the cleric, but subsequent information from Wilkes's records indicate that the chaplain was in such poor standing with his commander that he eventually resigned from the expedition, whereas the midshipman actually was a member of the survey party that explored the bay. [*See* Elliot Point.]

Ellisford (Okanogan). Named to honor two pioneer merchants in the Okanogan country, G. H. Ellis and J. E. Forde, partners in the Washington Commercial Co. stores.

Ellisport (King). Vashon Island community named in 1912 in honor of the Reverend Ellis, one of the early settlers in the area.

Elma (Grays Harbor). Named after Miss Elma Austin, early settler who was well known throughout the Puget Sound country.

Elmer City (Okanogan). The town was platted in 1937 and named to honor Elmer Seaton, operator of a Columbia River ferry prior to construction of Coulee Dam.

Elochoman River, ee-LOH-kuh-min (Wahkiakum). Known by a variety of names—Elochoman Slough, Alockaman and Elokamin

River—the stream, which joins the Columbia River near Cathlamet, derived its name from an Indian village, Ilhumin, situated
at its mouth.

Eltopia, el-TOHP-ee-uh (Franklin). Purportedly a euphonic contraction of "Hell-to-pay," the nickname given the site by a railroad
gang after heavy rains washed out the grade and delayed the construction schedule.

Elwha River, EL-wah (Clallam). Indian word meaning "elk."

Endicott (Whitman). The railroad station town was platted in 1882
by John O. Courtright, who named both the town and his son
(E. T. Courtright, born 1883) after a survey engineer of the
Oregon-Washington Railroad and Navigation Co.

Enetai, EN-a-teye (Kitsap). A Chinook jargon word meaning "crossing" or "across." The community, once called Port Orchard, was
a thriving lumber town operated by Capt. William Renton and
Daniel Howard, who moved their mill from Alki Point to the site.

Entiat, EN-tee-at (Chelan). The town situated at the junction of the
Entiat and Columbia rivers was named for the smaller stream in
1896. Entiat is an adaptation of the Indian name for the stream,
Enteatqua, meaning "rapid water."

Enumclaw, EE-nuhm-klaw (King). Named in 1885 by Frank Stevenson, original settler at the townsite, for a nearby mountain
called by the Indians "home of the evil spirits."

Ephrata, e-FRAY-tuh (Grant). The name is one of the alternates
used in the Bible for Bethlehem, the birthplace of Jesus. Ancient
meaning of the term is "fruit region," and since the site of the
future county seat boasted the only orchard in the area, it was
given the Hebrew name by railroad surveyors.

Espanola, es-puh-NOH-luh (Spokane). Name source unverified.
Purportedly the post office was known as Manilla in 1904 and subsequently changed to the present title.

Esperance, ES-per-awnce (Snohomish). Named by real estate developers Crawford and Conover for the latter's home town in New
York State.

Ethel (Lewis). The given name of his wife was assigned the town by Postmaster-General William F. Vilas in 1886.

Eunice Lake (Pierce). Located in the northwestern corner of Mt. Rainier National Park, the lake was initially named—as is the nearby peak—after Dr. William Fraser Tolmie, Hudson's Bay Company surgeon at Fort Nisqually and first white man to attempt the mountain's ascent. The lake was subsequently assigned the given name of Mrs. W. H. Gilstrap of Tacoma, a frequent visitor to the site. [*See* Tolmie Peak.]

Eureka, yoo-REE-kuh (Walla Walla). Platted in 1904 by Mrs. A. B. Blanchard as Eureka Flat, from the Greek exclamation, "I have found it!"

Evaline (Lewis). Named in 1906 for the wife of first postmaster Sedate W. Porter.

Evans (Stevens). Named in 1901 in honor of J. H. Evans, president of the Idaho Lime Co., which established a plant at the townsite.

Everett, EV-er-it (Snohomish). The county seat city was first platted in 1890 by Wyatt J. and Bethel J. Rucker as Port Gardner after the bay on which it is located. Rumors that the Great Northern Railroad might build a terminus at the timber-rich townsite caused the Rucker brothers to join forces with Tacoma lumber baron Henry Hewitt, Jr., and a group of eastern capitalists that included Charles L. Colby and John D. Rockefeller, in the Everett Land Co. In 1890 the city was incorporated under the name Everett in honor of promoter Colby's son. [*See* Possession Sound.]

Evergreen State. Official nickname of the state of Washington was suggested shortly after statehood by Charles T. Conover, pioneer Seattle real estate promoter.

Everson, EE-ver-suhn (Whatcom). Named in honor of Ever Everson, the first white settler in the area.

Ewan, EE-wahn (Whitman). Name source unverified. In 1861, Yakima Indian Chief Kamiakin, who had led the resistance against white settlers in the 1850s, returned from voluntary exile on the Crow Reservation and farmed in the Ewan area.

ℱ

Factoria (King). So named because it was planned and promoted as a manufacturing center on Lake Washington.

Fairchild (Spokane). Railway station and post office at Fairchild Air Force Base honor Gen. Muir S. Fairchild, vice chief of staff for air, who died while on Pentagon duty in March 1950.

Fairfield (Spokane). Named in 1888 by E. H. Morrison because the grain fields around the town reminded his wife of her eastern home town of that name.

Fall City (King). Platted in 1887 by Jeremiah Borst, first settler-storekeeper-postmaster, and so named because of its location below the falls of Snoqualmie River.

Farmington (Whitman). Named in 1878 by G. W. Truax for a town of the same name in his home state of Minnesota.

Fauntleroy Cove, FAWNT-luh-roi (King). The cove on Seattle's southwestern shore was named for love. In 1857, George Davidson of the U.S. Coast Survey was smitten with Ellinor Fauntleroy. To bolster his quest for her hand, he named his newly commissioned survey vessel for her father, Robert H. Fauntleroy, the cove for the brig (he claimed), and Olympic peaks—Mt. Ellinor, Mt. Constance, The Brothers, all of which are visible from the cove—for his fiancée, her sister, and her brothers, Arthur and Edward. Although he never bestowed a geographic honor on his mother-in-law, George and Ellinor were married in 1858.

Federal Way (King). Pacific Highway South (Route 99) was financed by United States government funds and, hence, was publicized as a "federal highway." A new school along the route was named Federal Way High School, and, in turn, the surrounding community subsequently adopted the name.

Felida, FA-lid-uh (Clark). Former town submitted the name Powley in honor of an old settler when petitioning for a post office. Postal authorities countered with Polly. The town fathers refused to have a parrot's name attached to their metropolis-to-be. C. C. Lewis, store clerk and ipso facto assistant postmaster, suggested Thomas after his cat. His fellow citizens derided his choice as being as unworthy as the government's. The quest for a distinctive name led to selection of the present title—an adaptation of the Latin word *felidae* for the cat genus—which had also been submitted by the piqued and persistent Lewis.

Ferndale (Whatcom). Named in 1872 by the first teacher because the town's new one-room log schoolhouse was situated in a fern patch.

Ferry County; 2,197 sq. mi.; 9th in size; seat: Republic. Established as a county on 21 February 1899 and named in honor of Seattleite Elisha P. Ferry, first governor of the state of Washington, 1889–93. Ferry had previously served as governor of Washington Territory, 1872–80, by appointment of President U. S. Grant. The initial bill called for the county to be designated as Eureka County.

Fidalgo Island, fi-DAL-goh (Skagit). Separated from the mainland by a narrow slough, this island was named for Salvadore Fidalgo of Eliza's exploration fleet of 1790. The name was assigned by Kellett in 1847 as part of his campaign of preserving early Spanish names. The actual discovery that the area was an island rather than part of the mainland was made by the Wilkes Expedition. Wilkes named the island in honor of Oliver Hazard Perry and its highest point for his victory in the Battle of Lake Erie in the War of 1812. Perry's Island is no more, but Mt. Erie still exists as a reminder of the man who cryptically announced his victory: "We have met the enemy and they are ours."

Fife (Pierce). Named after William Fife, Tacoma millionaire industrialist, who was instrumental in the community's development.

Finley (Benton). Named in honor of George Finley, early settler.

Fircrest (Pierce). Now a successful city with extra amenities, the community was initially platted in 1907 as Regents Park by Edward J. Bowes, who hosted the famed Amateur Hour during radio's golden era. A promotional flop, the development was incorporated in 1925, at which time, in hopes of a change in image, it adopted the name of the adjacent golf club.

Fisher (Clark). Named in 1881 for postmaster Solomon W. Fisher.

Flagler, Fort (Jefferson). Named in honor of Brig. Gen. Daniel Webster Flagler, Chief of Ordnance, U.S. Army, who died in 1899. [*See* Casey, Fort.]

Flattery, Cape (Clallam). The southern entrance of the Strait of Juan de Fuca and the northwestern extremity of Washington State was named indirectly by England's famed Capt. James Cook. On 22 March 1778 Cook entered in his journal that on shore "there appeared to be a small opening that flattered us with hopes of finding a harbour there"; closer examination proved the hopes to be in vain, so he named the point Cape Flattery. One of his lieutenants on the voyage—along with William Bligh of the subsequent *Bounty* mutiny—was George Vancouver, who upon his return to the region in command of an exploration expedition in 1792, ended the confusion as to the true location of Cook's Cape Flattery. He fixed it at its present location and charted the similar-appearing formation to the south as Flattery Rocks.

Flattery Rocks (Clallam). Rock formations off Cape Alava so named by Vancouver to differentiate them from the entrance to the Strait of Juan de Fuca, which Captain James Cook had named Cape Flattery in 1778.

Flattop Island (San Juan). Descriptive of the island's terrain, the name was chosen by Wilkes.

Florence (Snohomish). Named in 1884 by the first postmaster, F. E. Norton, for a former sweetheart.

Ford (Stevens). So named because it was the location of a ford across Tshimakain Creek in Walkers Prairie, site of a mission founded by Elkanah and Mary Walker and given the Indian name Tshimakain, meaning "plain of many springs."

Forks (Clallam). Town name originates because of its location near the forks of three rivers—the Calawah, Bogachiel, and Soleduck.

Fort Canby. *See* Canby, Fort.

Fort Casey. *See* Casey, Fort.

Fort Ebey. *See* Ebey, Fort.

Fort Flagler. *See* Flagler, Fort.

Fort Lawton. *See* Lawton, Fort.

Fort Lewis. *See* Lewis, Fort.

Fort Simcoe. *See* Simcoe, Fort.

Fortson, FORT-suhn (Snohomish). Named for Capt. George H. Fortson, an officer in the 1st Washington Infantry, who was killed in the Philippine War of 1899. He is also honored by a square at 2nd Ave. and Yesler Way in Seattle.

Fort Steilacoom. *See* Steilacoom, Fort.

Fort Worden. *See* Worden, Fort.

Fort Wright. *See* Wright, Fort.

Foster (King). Named for Joseph Foster, who homesteaded there in 1852.

Foulweather Bluff (Kitsap). Named by Vancouver because of rough weather he experienced off the eastern point of the entrance to Hood Canal.

Four Lakes (Spokane). So named because of the four small lakes in the area.

Fox Island (Pierce). Situated west of Tacoma, the island was named by Wilkes for J. L. Fox, one of the expedition's assistant surgeons.

Fragaria, fruh-GAIR-eeuh (Kitsap). The name is that of the genus to which the strawberry plant belongs and was chosen in 1914 by town platter Ferdinand Schmitz in recognition of the berry's successful growth in the area.

Frances (Pacific). Named by a Northern Pacific Railroad survey engineer after his wife.

Franklin (King). Former town in the Black Diamond–Franklin–Ravensdale coal field was named for the Franklin Coal Co. The name once was also that of present-day Puyallup.

Franklin County; 1,262 sq. mi.; 28th in size; seat: Pasco. Territorial legislature authorized county 28 November 1883 and named it in honor of Benjamin Franklin.

Frederickson (Pierce). Named for an early sawmill operator.

Freeland (Island). The town was first called Equality by its Socialist founders, who started a cooperative sawmill. The Freeland Colony, as the group was known, disbanded in 1904 when their property was sold to satisfy creditors.

Freeman (Spokane). Original railroad station named *circa* 1889 for telegrapher Truman W. Freeman.

Freeman Island (San Juan). West of Orcas Island; originally named Freeman's Island by Wilkes for J. D. Freeman, sailmaker aboard the expedition's *Peacock*.

Friday Harbor (San Juan). The county seat and main port of entry for San Juan Island took its name from Friday, an aged Kanaka sheepherder brought to the island from Hawaii by the Hudson's Bay Co. to tend its flock.

Friday Island (San Juan). Local name for a small island at the entrance to Friday Harbor, San Juan Island. [*See* Brown Island.]

Frost Island (San Juan). Wilkes named the island for John Frost, boatswain of the expedition's *Porpoise*.

Fruitland (Stevens). Initially known as Robbers' Roost, an infamous hideout for cattle rustlers, the small orchard community was established in 1880 and known variously as Spring Valley, Price's Valley, and Fruitland Valley. In 1887 a post office was requested, these names were submitted, and postal authorities picked the present title.

Furport (Pend Oreille). Established and named in 1924 by Joseph C. Grover, storekeeper and rabbit rancher, who constructed an artificial pond by the Pend Oreille River for muskrat raising.

Galvin (Lewis). Platted and named Lincoln in 1910 by the Galvin Teal Co., the town was renamed for its cofounder John Galvin, mayor of Centralia.

Gardiner (Jefferson). Originally called Gardner after Herbert Gardner, who settled the townsite area in 1906. Subsequently, the name was changed to Gardiner to avoid confusion with another Gardner post office in the state.

Gardner, Port (Snohomish). The harbor of the city of Everett was named on 4 June 1792 by Vancouver in honor of Sir Alan Gardner, vice admiral of the British Navy. He named the southern tip of Camano Island as Alan Point (later known as Allen Point) for his friend, and the waterway to the north for the admiral's wife, Lady Susana. [*See* Possession Sound.]

Garfield (Whitman). Named in June 1882 by town platter and first postmaster S. J. Tant in honor of President James A. Garfield, who had been assassinated the previous fall.

Garfield County; 714 sq. mi.; 33rd in size; seat: Pomeroy. Name honors President James A. Garfield. The county was established by the territorial legislature on 29 November 1881.

Garrison Bay (San Juan). The small bay on the northwestern coast of San Juan Island was near the site of English Camp manned by British soldiers during the San Juan border dispute.

Gate (Thurston). Originally called Gate City, as it is situated at a narrow end of a valley and was considered the gateway to the Grays Harbor country.

Gedney Island (Snohomish). Situated between Everett and Whidbey Island, the island was officially charted by Wilkes as Gedney Island for a friend, presumably inventor Jonathon Haight Gedney of New York. However, because of its appearance it is often locally known—and charted on some maps—as Hat Island. [*See* Hat Island.]

Geneva (Whatcom). Community on the shore of Lake Whatcom was so named in 1882 by David C. Jenkins for its Swiss counterpart.

George (Grant). Named by the town's first mayor Charles Brown, a Quincy businessman, who bought the townsite from the U.S. Reclamation Bureau. Dedicated on 4 July 1957, the city's streets are lined with cherry trees and are named after different types of cherry trees.

Georgia Strait. This northern boundary between San Juan County, U.S.A., and Canada was named by Vancouver in honor of the King of England. On 4 June 1792 Vancouver celebrated the birthday of George III by taking possession of the region he was exploring. The ceremony took place near the present site of the city of Everett. He named the harbor there Possession Sound, bestowed the name Gulf of Georgia on Puget Sound, and claimed the mainland "binding the said gulf, and extending southward to the 45th degree of north latitude." He called the region "New Georgia, in honor of His present Majesty." [*See* Possession Sound.]

Gifford (Stevens). Named for James O. Gifford, who settled in the area in 1890.

Gig Harbor (Pierce). Town on the southeastern shore of Kitsap Peninsula derived its name from the small harbor named by Wilkes because it "has sufficient depth of water for small vessels."

Ginkgo Petrified Forest, GINK-goh (Kittitas). A part of a ginkgo tree forest that existed 10,000,000 years ago, the state park features more than 200 varieties of petrified flora. Wild ginkgo trees are extinct, but species of the "sacred tree of China," known as silver apricot and temple trees, still exist in the Orient.

Glacier (Whatcom). Situated on and named for Glacier Creek, which was named for a glacier on nearby Mt. Baker.

Gleed (Yakima). Railway shipping point was initially called Gleed Siding after hay farmer James Gleed, on whose property the siding and then the railroad station were built.

Glen Cove (Jefferson). Port Townsend Bay settlement was platted as a summer home community and named after the fashionable summer resort on Long Island, N.Y.

Glenoma, glen-OH-muh (Lewis). Literally "fruitful valley," as it is a coined name composed of the Scottish word *glen,* meaning "small valley," and the old Hebrew word *oma,* meaning "a measure of grain."

Glenwood (Klickitat). So named because it was situated in a small valley surrounded by forests.

Gold Bar (Snohomish). Prospectors searching for gold along the Skykomish River and its tributaries in 1869 gave the name to the region. The town was platted and formally named in 1900 by the Gold Bar Improvement Co.

Goldendale (Klickitat). County seat was named after John J. Golden, who, in 1863, homesteaded the site that became the town in 1872.

Goodnoe Hills (Klickitat). In the early 1900s a rural post office and railroad station were named after Chauncey Goodnoe, who established a ranch along the Columbia River in 1865.

Goose Island (San Juan). Goose, Buck, and Long islands and Whale and Mummy rocks in Davis Bay southwest of Lopez Island were all charted by Wilkes under the single name of Goose Island. The present names were first shown on the British Admiralty charts of 1848.

Gooseprairie (Yakima). The natural meadow on the Bumping River was so named in the 1860s by Scots immigrants John and Tom Fife for a lone goose that settled on their homestead.

Gorst (Kitsap). Named after early settler Samuel Gorst.

Govan, goh-VAN (Lincoln). Named for an engineer of the old Washington Central Railroad.

Graham (Pierce). Town bears the name of a woods boss, as mail and freight destined for the logging camp was sent "c/o Mr. Graham."

Grand Coulee, KOO-lee (Grant). So named, as is nearby Coulee City, because of its location in the gigantic coulee that was the bed of the Columbia River in past ages.

Grand Coulee Dam (Grant). Authorized by President Franklin D. Roosevelt as part of the Public Works Administration program, Bureau of Reclamation construction of the dam began in 1933. The first electricity was transmitted in 1941, and the first irrigation water flowed in 1951. The dam across the Columbia River in the Grand Coulee created a tremendous recreation area and several construction towns, most important of which are Coulee Dam, Grand Coulee, Electric City, and Elmer City.

Grand Mound (Thurston). The town is situated in Mound Prairie, which is characterized by peculiar symmetrical humps of earth. The town is located near the largest of the mounds, a 125-foot-high hillock covered with trees, hence the name.

Grandview (Yakima). Founded in 1906 and named for its panoramic view of Mt. Adams and Mt. Rainier.

Granger (Yakima). Established in 1902, the town was named for Walter N. Granger, president of the Sunnyside Canal Co., one of the first irrigation projects in the state. Granger also promoted the nearby towns of Sunnyside and Zillah.

Granite Falls (Snohomish). Named for the falls in a granite rock canyon of the Stillaguamish River.

Grant County; 2,691 sq. mi.; 4th in size; seat: Ephrata. County authorized by state law 24 February 1909 and named in honor of President Ulysses S. Grant. [*See* Lincoln County.]

Grant Orchards (Grant). The name applies to the railroad station at Soap Lake in the heart of Grant County's fruit-growing district.

Grapeview (Mason). Platted in 1891 as Detroit, the town was subsequently renamed, as it faces the vineyards of the Isle of Grapes. [*See* Stretch Island.]

Grayland (Grays Harbor). Named as a tie in to its position at the southeastern end of Grays Harbor County when the town was established by Finnish cranberry growers.

Grays (Stevens). Former town on the Colville River was named after an early settler.

Grays Harbor. Discovered 7 May 1792 by Capt. Robert Gray and named Bullfinch Harbor in honor of one of the Boston owners of his ship *Columbia Rediviva*. In October of the same year, the harbor was surveyed by Joseph Whidbey of the Vancouver Expedition and renamed Gray's Harbor to honor its discoverer. Rhode Island-born Gray, who served as a privateer in the Revolutionary War, visited the Pacific Northwest coast in 1787–90 and again in 1790–93 on fur-trading ventures. His voyages and discoveries were the foundation of American claim to the Oregon country. [*See* Columbia River.]

Grays Harbor County; 1,905 sq. mi.; 15th in size; seat: Montesano. Established as Chehalis County by territorial legislature in 1854. In 1907, the state legislature approved division of the county into two parts, to be known as Chehalis County and Grays Harbor County. However, the state supreme court ruled against the act, and in 1915 the legislature changed the name of the whole to Grays Harbor County honoring explorer Robert Gray, the first American to sail around the world.

Grays River (Wahkiakum). The town was named for the river of the same name which, in turn, was named for the bay into which it flows. Grays Bay on the Columbia River honors Capt. Robert Gray.

Greenacres (Spokane). So named because it was originally a community of truck garden tracts.

Greenbank (Island). Named by an early settler for his boyhood home town of Green Bank, Del.

Grenville, Point (Grays Harbor). In 1775 Capt. Bruno Heceta anchored his vessel *Santiago* near Point Grenville and went ashore to claim the land in the name of the King of Spain and, thus, became the first white man to land on the shores of the present state of Washington. Heceta called the spot Punta de los Martires, or "Point of the Martyrs," because of an Indian attack. On 28 April 1792 Vancouver gave the point its present name to honor Lord William Wyndham Grenville, a cousin of William Pitt.

Griffin Bay (San Juan). The shallow harbor on the southeastern coast of San Juan Island was named in 1858 for British colonial justice of the peace Charles John Griffin, the Hudson's Bay Co. official in charge of Bellevue Farm. [*See* San Juan County.]

Grotto (King). Name derived from the many deep gorges in the area that appear to be caves when observed from a distance.

Guemes Island, GWAY-muhs (Skagit). Named Isla de Guemes in honor of the viceroy of Mexico by the Spanish exploration of 1791–92 under Eliza.

Guss Island (San Juan). The small island in Garrison Bay on the northwestern shore of San Juan Island was named for Guss Hoffmaster, a German who ran a store catering to English soldiers at English Camp during the dispute over the American-Canadian boundary.

H

Hadlock (Jefferson). Originally known as Port Hadlock, the town was named for founder Samuel Hadlock, who built the Washington Mill Co. sawmill on Port Townsend Bay in 1870.

Hale Passage (Pierce). Situated between Fox Island and the mainland, the waterway was named by Wilkes for Horatio Hale, the expedition's philologist. Hale remained in the Oregon country when the expedition returned to New York and was the first man to compile a formal Chinook jargon dictionary.

Hamilton (Skagit). Named for early settler William Hamilton.

Hamilton Island (Skamania). Island, mountain, small tributary to the Columbia River, and a former post office all derive their name from Samuel Milton Hamilton, an early donation claim settler on the creek.

Hamma Hamma River, HAM-uh-HAM-uh (Mason). The river carries a phonetic corruption of *Hab'hab,* the name of a Twana Indian village at its mouth on Hood Canal. The Indian word *hab-hab* or *hub-hub* is the name of a reed that grows along the swampy portions of the river's banks.

Hammersley Inlet (Mason). The southwestern arm of Puget Sound that leads to Shelton was named by Wilkes for one of the expedition's midshipmen, George W. Hammersly, who spelled his name with one less *e* than did his commander or subsequent government mapmakers.

Hammond, Point (San Juan). The northeastern tip of Waldron Island was named by Wilkes for Henry Hammond, one of the expedition's quartermasters.

Hanbury Point (San Juan). The point on the western shore of San Juan Island was named by Capt. Daniel Pender in 1869 to honor Ingram Hanbury, royal naval surgeon who served the nearby British camp during the boundary dispute.

Hanford (Benton). The town was named in 1906 by the Hanford Irrigation and Power Co. for its president-founder, Seattleite Cornelius H. Hanford, the first federal judge in the state. The town and nearby community of White Bluffs, centers for early-crop strawberries and watermelons, were vacated when the government purchased 193,833 acres in 1943 for construction of the Hanford Works, plutonium-producing plant of the Atomic Energy Commission. [*See* Tri-Cities.]

Hansville (Kitsap). The resort community between Norwegian Point and Point No Point on northern Kitsap Peninsula was named for early settler Hans Zachariason.

Harney Channel (San Juan). The passage between Orcas and Shaw islands was named by the British for U.S. Army Brig. Gen. William S. Harney who sent Company D of the 9th Infantry under Capt. George E. Pickett to protect Americans living on British-claimed San Juan Island. The action on 9 July 1859 precipitated the "Pig War" that resulted in joint occupancy until 1870.

Haro Strait, HAIR-oh. The western waterway between the San Juan Islands and Vancouver Island honors Spanish sailing master Lopez Gonzales de Haro, reputedly the first discoverer of the San Juans. Haro Strait connects the Strait of Juan de Fuca with the Strait of Georgia, and the three are traversed by the United States–Canadian boundary.

Harper (Kitsap). The town on the south shore of Yukon Harbor was renamed in 1902 for state senator F. C. Harper, whose influence was instrumental in securing a post office at that location. The action was taken despite the protests of a strong minority that urged retention of the original name of Terra Vaughn.

Harrah, HAIR-uh (Yakima). The reservation town was established in 1913 as Saluskin in honor of Chief Saluskin of the Yakima tribe. In 1915, it was renamed for J. T. Harrah, operator of the area's largest ranch and the community's main source of income. Until his death in 1917, the chief berated the business pressure that caused the switch in names and referred to the community as Thief Town.

Harrington (Lincoln). Named in 1882 for Colusa, Calif., banker W. P. Harrington, who invested heavily in land in the area.

Hartline (Grant). Named after John Hartline, who homesteaded the land on which the town stands.

Hartstene Island, HAHRT-steen (Mason). Named by Wilkes for Lt. Henry J. Hartstene of the expedition. The muster roll of the expedition shows the name as Hartstein, and early government and state maps spelled the name Hartstine. The island community has been known variously as Harstine and Harstene.

Hat Island (Skagit). The small island off the southeast tip of Guemes Island was initially charted as Peacock Island by Wilkes to honor one of the expedition's five vessels. Because of its shape, it was renamed Hat Island in 1904 by the U.S. Coast Survey. The change often results in confusion with another Wilkes-named island—Gedney Island west of Everett in Snohomish County, which is known locally (and unofficially on some charts) as Hat Island. [*See* Gedney Island.]

Hatton (Adams). Originally known as Twin Wells because of the existence of railroad water wells, the town was retitled with establishment of a post office in 1888. The name was a composite coined from the names of railroad agent, J. D. *Ha*ckett, and his bride, Belle Su*tton,* who served as first postmistress.

Havermale Island (Spokane). The huge rock in the Spokane River just above Spokane Falls was named for the Reverend S. G. Havermale, early Spokane minister. During the Nez Perce Indian uprising of 1877, settlers within a 25-mile radius took refuge on the midstream safety of the island.

Havillah, ha-VIL-uh (Okanogan). Name selected in 1905 by storekeeper and gristmill operator Martin H. Schweikert from the Bible, Genesis II:5-11.

Hay (Whitman). During the blizzard winter of 1892-93, a railroad siding at the site was identified simply as "hay station" because of the quantities of hay shipped in to feed cattle. As a community developed and a post office was secured, the latter word was deemed superfluous.

Heisson, HEYE-suhn (Clark). Named in honor of Alexander and Marie Heisson, German immigrants who settled at the townsite in 1867.

Henderson Inlet (Thurston). Named by Wilkes in honor of the expedition's quartermaster, James Henderson.

Henry Island (San Juan). Named by Wilkes for Midshipman Wilkes Henry, a nephew of the commander, who had been killed by natives in the Fiji Islands while the squadron was en route to the Pacific Northwest. [*See* Vendovi Island; Viti Rocks.]

Herron Island, HAIR-on (Pierce). The small island in Case Inlet was named by Wilkes for petty officer Lewis Herron, the expedition's cooper (barrel maker).

Hobart (King). Exact name source unknown. Records indicate that the post office was established in 1888 and named for a prominent—but unremembered—territorial figure.

Hockinson, HAHK-in-suhn (Clark). The community name is an anglicized spelling of the name of early Swedish settler, Ambrosius Hokanson.

Hoh River, HOH (Jefferson). River flowing from Mt. Olympus to the Pacific, Hoh Head north of the river mouth, Hoh Peak west of Mt. Olympus, and the Hoh Indian Reservation bear the name of a band of Indians of the Quillayute tribe. [*See* Destruction Island.]

Holcomb (Pacific). Honors Judge George Holcomb, first mayor of nearby South Bend, who was active in the South Bend Land Co. during the boom of 1890.

Holden (Chelan). Named for James Henry Holden, who made the initial copper-gold-zinc strike in 1896 that led to establishment of the Howe Sound Mining Co. mine and town. Following closure of the mine, the town was purchased by the Lutheran Church for a religious retreat village.

Holly (Kitsap). Named in 1895 by Robert Wyatt for a large holly tree near the post office.

Holmes Harbor (Island). Named by Wilkes for the expedition's assistant surgeon, Silas Holmes. The Indian name for the bay was *ah-lus-dukh*, meaning "go inside."

Home (Pierce). Established as a social reform colony in 1896 on Carr Inlet by George H. Allen and named to demonstrate the group's friendship to all.

Home Valley (Skamania). A Norwegian settlement which first postmaster John Kanekeberg named Heim Dal and which postal authorities translated to its present title in 1893.

Hood Canal. The 80-mile-long tidal channel separating Kitsap and Olympic peninsulas was named on Sunday, 13 May 1792, by Vancouver in honor of The Right Honorable Lord Samuel Hood. He entered it in his journal as Hood's Channel, but on his charts as Hood's Canal. The U.S. Geographic Board resolved the dilemma by adopting the present spelling. A vicar's son, Samuel Hood (1724–1816) was an admiral in the British Navy who received much of his fame for victories against United States vessels in the Revolutionary War. He was called "the Englishman who won the war for the colonies" because of his failure to pick up Cornwallis' troops as prearranged, thereby leaving the general to defeat in the decisive battle at Yorktown.

Hoodsport (Mason). Townsite, originally called Slal-atl-atl-tul-hu by the Twana Indians, took its name from Hood Canal, as did Hood Head, north of Port Gamble, in Jefferson County. However, the small town of Hood in Skamania County takes its name from towering Mt. Hood across the Columbia River in Oregon, which was also named for Lord Samuel Hood by the Vancouver Expedition.

Hoogdal, HOHG-dahl (Skagit). Named by early settlers after their former home in the Ytter-Hogdahl district of Sweden.

Hooper (Whitman). Named in honor of pioneer rancher A. J. Hooper.

Hoquiam, HOH-kwee-uhm (Grays Harbor). Older and smaller than its abutting neighbor Aberdeen, the city was settled in 1859 by the James Karr family, and the present name was applied to both settlement and river. The name is a contraction of the Indian term *ho-qui-umpts,* meaning "hungry for wood," and refers to the driftwood at the river's mouth.

Horse Heaven Hills. Until the middle of the twentieth century the parched, rugged hills between the Yakima and Columbia rivers from Satus Pass to Kennewick were a sanctuary for bands of wild horses forced from low pasture by establishment of homestead farms.

Houghton, HOH-tuhn (King). Town on Lake Washington that merged with Kirkland in the late 1960s was originally named for logger Willard Houghton, who settled there in 1875.

Huckleberry Island (Skagit). Descriptive name assigned by U.S. Coast and Geodetic Survey in 1904. [*See* Dot Island.]

Humptulips, huhm-TOO-lips (Grays Harbor). The river and a town on its banks derive their names from an Indian term meaning "chilly region." Some sources indicate that the translation is "hard to pole"—with either term appropriately fitting the river.

Hunters (Stevens). Both the town and nearby creek honor James Hunter, the first white settler at the location.

Hunts Point (King). Township on the east shore of Lake Washington was named for Leigh S. J. Hunt, a former publisher of the Seattle *Post-Intelligencer* newspaper, who had extensive land holdings in the area.

Huntsville (Columbia). Named for the pioneer Hunt family.

Husum, HYOO-suhm (Klickitat). Named in 1880 after Husum, Germany, home town of many of the early settlers.

Hyak, HEYE-ak (Kittitas). Community at the east portal of the railway tunnel through the Cascade Mountains bears the Chinook jargon word meaning "hurry."

Hyde Point (Pierce). The eastern cape of McNeil Island was named by Wilkes for the expedition's William Hyde, carpenter's mate.

i

Iceberg Island (San Juan). The name comes from nearby Iceberg Point on Lopez Island that was so named by the U.S. Coast Survey of 1854 because of "remarkable deep and smooth marks of glacial action."

Illahee, il-LAH-hee (Kitsap). A Chinook jargon word meaning "earth" or "country."

Ilwaco, il-WAH-koh (Pacific). A salmon-fishing town near the mouth of the Columbia River named to honor Chinook Indian sub-chief El-wah-ko, it was originally established as Unity by Isaac Whealdon in 1868.

Image (Clark). Suburb of Vancouver was named for an island in the Columbia River called Image Canoe Island by Lewis and Clark.

Inchelium, in-chuh-LEE-uhm (Ferry). An Indian name for the site, meaning "surrounded by water."

Index (Snohomish). Town named for nearby mountain, which was so named because of a sharp pinnacle at its top that resembles an index finger.

Indianola, IN-deeuhn-o-la (Kitsap). Named Indianola Beach in 1916 by a development company because the land was originally an allotment grant to a member of the Port Madison band of Indians. Postal authorities rejected the double-word name and called the post office Kitsap after the Indian chief. In the late 1950s the post office name was changed to Indianola, the one-word, common-usage name for the community.

Inglewood (King). Although it is a popular town name in England, Canada, and the eastern United States, the reason for its adoption by the north Lake Washington community is unverified.

Ione, eye-OHN (Pend Oreille). Named on 1 April 1896 for Ione Morrison, niece of the town's first postmaster and daughter of its second.

Irby (Lincoln). Named after early settler John Irby.

Irondale (Jefferson). Community at the mouth of Chimacum Creek on Port Townsend Bay was the site of a short-lived iron works erected by Western Steel Corp. The name of the resultant boom town was chosen because of iron ore bogs in the vicinity. However, the blast furnace produced pig iron from Chinese ore.

Irvin (Spokane). Settled in 1847 by Spokane River ferryman Antoine La Plante (whose sons-in-law have as their namesakes Newman and Liberty lakes). Chronologically, the site was called Cliffton, because of an overhanging canyon rim, Myrtle's Point, Trent, and Louisville (by a brewery for promotional value). Its present name was assigned in 1912 to honor a major stockholder of the nearby Portland Cement Co. plant.

Island County; 206 sq. mi.; 38th in size; seat: Coupeville. Organized by the Oregon Territorial Legislature on 6 January 1853 and so named because it consists solely of islands: Whidbey, Camano, Ben Ure, Smith, Deception, and Hackney.

Issaquah, IS-uh-kwah (King). Derived from the Indian word *is-quowh* of uncertain meaning, the name is currently that of a town, a creek, a mountain, and a valley. Originally the town was known as Squak, a corruption of the Indian name; next as Gilman for coal-mine operator D. H. Gilman. It was also known as Olney and Englewood before settlers agreed to the present name in 1890.

J

James Island (Clallam). An island offshore from La Push on the Quillayute Indian Reservation with 200-foot perpendicular bluffs and only one narrow path to the top. The Quillayutes used it as a fortress to ward off raiding Makah warriors from Neah Bay. When attacked, the Quillayutes would retreat to the top and dump rocks and boiling water on enemy braves attempting to climb the trail. Originally called Ah-kah-laht, "way up there," the island has been renamed by the Indians to honor Chief Jimmy Howe.

James Island (San Juan). This name represents another of Wilkes's tie-in names, this time to nearby Decatur Island. When Stephen Decatur burned the U.S.S. *Philadelphia* in Tripoli Harbor, his brother James was slain by a Barbary vessel which had feigned surrender. Enraged, Decatur boarded the pirate vessel and while engaged in hand-to-hand combat was saved from death by Reuben James, an American sailor who took a Turk's scimitar slash meant for the lieutenant.

Jared, JAIR-ed (Pend Oreille). Named for pioneer storekeeper Robert P. Jared.

Jefferson County; 1,812 sq. mi.; 18th in size; seat: Port Townsend. Named in honor of President Thomas Jefferson by the Oregon Territorial Legislature on 22 December 1852.

John Day Dam (Klickitat). Name results from the Columbia River dam's location immediately downstream from the mouth of Oregon's John Day River. The latter was named for Virginia backwoodsman John Day, a member of John Jacob Astor's Pacific Fur Co. Expedition. Day and a companion became separated from the main party during the winter of 1811–12 and were robbed naked by hostile Indians near the mouth of the stream. Left to die of starvation and exposure, the two men were eventually rescued and returned to Astoria.

Johnson (Whitman). Named for Jonathan Johnson, who settled the townsite in 1877.

Jones Island (San Juan). Named by Wilkes in honor of Jacob Jones, captain of the sloop-of-war *Wasp* when it was captured by the British brig *Frolic* in the War of 1812. [*See* Wasp Island.]

Jovita, joh-VEE-tuh (Pierce). The former townsite was developed by the Jovita Land Co. of Seattle, which explains the use of the Spanish feminine given name [correctly pronounced HOH-vee-tuh].

Joyce (Clallam). Named in 1913 by its first postmaster J. M. Joyce, who also operated a store, a shingle mill, and a farm in and near the community.

Juan de Fuca, Strait of, WAHN-de-FYOO-cuh. The waterway that forms the international boundary between Vancouver Island and the Olympic Peninsula and joins Puget Sound to the Pacific Ocean was seen and named, but not explored, by English Capt. Charles William Barclay of the *Imperial Eagle* in 1787. In June of 1788 another Englishman, Capt. John Meares, examined the entrance and also charted it with the name of its alleged discoverer: Juan de Fuca. The latter was actually a Greek navigator named Apostolos Valerianos, who purportedly spent 40 years sailing under the Spanish flag and a Spanish alias. In 1596 English merchant Michael Lok heard the old seaman's geographically detailed account of having discovered and sailed through the Straits of Anian —the long-sought Northwest Passage between the Pacific and Atlantic oceans. Lok passed on to mapmakers the old man's yarn of sailing north from Mexico along unexplored shores of western America in 1592 and finding the entrance "between 47 and 48 degrees Latitude." The story received some credence, although Vancouver and later historians, who helped perpetuate the use of Juan de Fuca's name, personally doubted its truth. Subsequent research of official archives in Mexico and Spain failed to disclose a record of the old seaman under either of his names or of the ships he claimed to have crewed for the viceroy of Mexico.

Juanita, waw-NEE-tuh (King). The community on the northeastern shore of Lake Washington was originally a sawmill site called Hubbard for early settler and first postmaster Martin W. Hubbard. Following closure of the post office in 1905, the bay and beach converted to a summer residence and resort area called Juanita. Why the Spanish girl's name came into existence is unverified, but it was the official name of a new post office when the Juanita township was platted in 1921.

K

Kachess Lake, kuh-CHEES (Kittitas). Indian word meaning "more fish," in contrast to the neighboring Keechelus Lake, meaning "few fish."

Kahlotus, kuh-LOH-tuhs (Franklin). The town name is an Indian word meaning "hole-in-the-ground."

Kalaloch, KLAY-lahk (Jefferson). Quinault Indian term meaning "sheltered landing" for canoes at the site's freshwater lagoon.

Kalama, kuh-LAM-uh (Cowlitz). Gen. J. W. Sprague of the Northern Pacific Railroad named the town in 1871 for the Indian word *calama,* meaning "pretty maiden."

Kamilche, kuh-MIL-chee (Mason). A corruption of the Indian word *ka-bel-chi,* meaning "valley."

Kanasket, kuh-NAS-kuht (King). Town carries the name of the hostile Indian chief who was killed by troops under Lt. William A. Slaughter during the Indian Wars of 1855–56. [*See* Auburn.]

Kapowsin, kuh-POW-suhn (Pierce). The town's first title of Hall was changed in 1903 to identify it geographically with its location on the northwestern shore of the lake called Kapousen by the Indians.

Keechelus Lake, KECH-uh-lus (Kittitas). Indian word meaning "few fish," in contrast to nearby Lake Kachess, which carries the name for "more fish."

Keller (Ferry). The town on the Sanpoil River was named for merchant J. C. Keller, who set up his first store in a tent in 1898.

Kellett Bluff (San Juan). The southern tip of Henry Island, and Kellett Ledge off the southeastern coast of Lopez Island, were named by the British and Americans, respectively, in honor of British Navy Capt. Henry Kellett of the surveying vessel *Herald*. Kellett charted the waters in 1847 and adjusted earlier name assignments in an attempt to clarify duplications and preserve historical priorities. [*See* San Juan Islands.]

Kelso (Cowlitz). County seat was platted and named by Peter W. Crawford for his home town in Scotland.

Kendall (Whatcom). Named for Carthage Kendall, a Virginian who settled on the north fork of the Nooksack River in 1884.

Kenmore (King). Shingle tycoon John McMaster named the site of his mill for his childhood home of Kenmore, Ont., Canada, which is the namesake of a village on the River Tay in Scotland.

Kennewick, KEN-uh-wik (Benton). The town name, derived from an Indian word *kin-i-wack,* meaning "grassy place," was given in 1883 by H. S. Huson of the Northern Pacific Irrigation Co. [*See* Tri-Cities.]

Kennydale (King). Community was platted *circa* 1903 in residential lots and two-acre tracts as the "Garden of Eden Addition to Seattle" by C. D. Hillman. "Kenny" was the surname of Hillman's son-in-law (or, according to some sources, his wife's maiden name). The nearby railroad section house of Quendall was once Port Quendall, the shipping point for coal from Newcastle to Seattle.

Kent (King). Originally called Titusville after early settler James H. Titus, the town was initially two separate communities. One was platted in 1884 by Henry L. Yesler, Seattle's first sawmill operator, and the other in 1888 by John Alexander and Ida L. Guiberson. Desirous of properly naming its station, the Northern Pacific Railroad consulted pioneer writer-promoter Ezra Meeker, the area's leading hop grower. With an eye to the sale of hop starters to new settlers, Meeker suggested that the "Hop Capital of the West" be called Kent after England's hop-growing center.

Ketron Island (Pierce). The island southwest of Steilacoom was named by Wilkes—but misspelled by his cartographers—for William Kittson, who supervised construction of Fort Nisqually for the Hudson's Bay Co. [*See* Nisqually.]

Kettle Falls (Stevens). This town, destined to be flooded by the backwater of Coulee Dam, was relocated four miles north of its original site by consolidating with the smaller community of Meyers Falls. The town is named for nearby Kettle Falls on the Columbia River. Two languages, Indian and French, gave birth to its name. The Indians called the falls Ilth-kapc, meaning "tightly woven cooking basket" and "net," as they fished there with such kettle-nets. The French traders called the falls La Chaudière because the water boiled like water in a heated pot or cauldron. Both terms were quickly translated by early settlers into the present name for the falls and river, and eventually the town.

Kewa, KEE-wuh (Ferry). Name source unverified.

Keyport (Kitsap). Builders of the community's first wharf gave it the name of a New Jersey town which they had picked at random from an atlas because they felt that it would become the key port on Liberty Bay. It is now the site of the Keyport Naval Torpedo Station.

Kilisut Harbor, KIL-i-suht (Jefferson). Enclosed deep-water harbor formed by Marrowstone and Indian islands bears the Clallam Indian term meaning "protected waters."

King County; 2,134 sq. mi.; 12th in size; seat: Seattle. Established by the Oregon Territorial Legislature on 22 December 1852 and named in honor of William Rufus DeVane King. Former senator from Alabama, minister to France, and acting vice president of the United States (upon the death of Zachary Taylor and the succession of Millard Fillmore), King died in 1853 before he actually took office. King and Pierce counties were carved out of Thurston County in 1852 and named for President-elect Franklin Pierce and Vice President-elect King.

Kingston (Kitsap). A contraction of King's Town adopted in 1890 by townsite platters, Mr. and Mrs. C. C. Calkins, who were the principals of the Kingston Land Development Co. The word "King" in various ways was used locally for some years to identify the area geographically, as it had been the base of logging operations for a lumberman with that surname.

Kiona, KEE-oh-nuh (Benton). Originally named Horseshoe Bend for its location on a nearly U-shaped bend in the Yakima River, the present name is an Indian word meaning "brown hills."

Kirkland (King). Named in honor of Peter Kirk, English millionaire who founded the town in 1886 in hopes of developing it into a steel manufacturing center.

Kitsap County, KIT-sap; 402 sq. mi.; 36th in size; seat: Port Orchard. Established by the territorial legislature 16 January 1857 as Slaughter County in honor of Lt. W. A. Slaughter, who was killed by Indians in 1855. [*See* Auburn.] At the next general election the citizens voted to rename it for Kitsap, a local war chief and medicine man who fought against the settlers in the Indian wars of 1855–56. While confined to the Fort Steilacoom guardhouse awaiting trial on murder charges for his part in the uprising, Kitsap was taken ill and treated with a red-colored liquid. Following his acquittal and release, he added "red magic medicine" made of red paint to his cures. His next three patients died. Their relatives swore vengeance, and on 18 April 1860 the drunken chief was shot and hacked into pieces. The Indians pronounce it *k'tsap,* as if the *i* were omitted, with heavy accent on the last syllable; the name means "brave."

Kittitas, KIT-i-tas (Kittitas). Established as a railway station and named after the Kittitas Valley by H. R. Williams.

Kittitas County; 2,315 sq. mi.; 8th in size; seat: Ellensburg. County established by the territorial legislature on 24 November 1883. The name is derived from the K'tatas Indian tribe or "shoal people," who lived along the shallow portion of the Yakima River.

Klickitat, KLIK-i-tat (Klickitat). Prior to renaming in 1910, the town was called Wrights after 1890 settler L. C. Wright.

Klickitat County; 1,912 sq. mi.; 14th in size; seat: Goldendale. The territorial legislature established Clickitat [*sic*] County on 20 December 1859. In the same year the surveyor-general of the territory charted the county's main stream, which rises from a glacier on Mt. Adams, as the Klickatat [*sic*] River. In addition to various spellings, the Indian name for the tribe that resided in the south-central area of the state has been given various meanings, including "robber" and "beyond." The latter is generally the more accepted definition, as it is the Chinook term having reference to the Cascade Mountains. However, either term fits the Klickitats' role as midway resident traders and intermediaries between the coastal tribes (Chinook) and those east of the mountains (Yakimas and Toppenish).

Klipsan Beach, KLIP-suhn (Pacific). An Indian word meaning "sunset" was assigned in 1912 by Capt. Theodore Conick of the coast guard station at the site.

Kosmos, KAHZ-muhs (Lewis). Named with the Greek word *kosmos,* meaning "the world," by Tacoma attorney B. W. Coiner in 1910. Townsite inundated by waters of the Mossyrock Dam's Riffe Lake in 1968. [*See* Riffe Lake.]

Krupp (Grant). Corporate town name for the post office of Marlin.

Kula Kala Point, KUH-la KAH-la (Clallam). A point east of Dungeness is a misspelling of the Chinook jargon word *kula kula,* meaning "travel."

L

La Center (Clark). Originally a river port known as Timmen's Landing, the town was platted in 1875 on the claim of John H. Timmen. Its position as focal point of both river and wagon-road traffic led to its present name as its developers foresaw it as "the center" of commerce for the area.

Lacey (Thurston). Originally known as Woodland after Isaac Woods, who settled the area in 1852, the community boasted two large sawmills, a resort hotel, the region's biggest horse-racing track, and a 10-by-12-foot log schoolhouse in the 1890s. Believing the prestige of a post office would stimulate further growth, Woods submitted a petition through his attorney, O. C. Lacey of Olympia. Postal officials rejected the railroad station name of Woodland as duplicating a town name in Cowlitz County. So Lacey, who doubled as real estate developer and who had land interests in the area, substituted his own name on the application to expedite matters. Incorporated in 1966, the city is the site of St. Martin's [Catholic] College.

La Conner (Skagit). The town, which straddles the Swinomish Slough, was the site of a trading post established in 1867 by Alonzo Lowe, one of the Alki Point pioneers. In 1869 he sold out to John S. Conner, who changed the post office name from Swinomish to La Conner after his wife, Louise Anne (Siegfried) Conner by using the initials of her first and middle names as a prefix to her last name.

Lacrosse (Whitman). Named by two construction engineers who surveyed the first railroad line through the area. One was from La Crosse, Wis., and the other from Winona, Minn., so they named two consecutive railway stations on the Union Pacific line for their respective home towns. *La crosse* is the name applied to a ball-and-racquet game originated by North American Indians.

La Grande (Pierce). Originally, French-Canadians of the Hudson's Bay Co. titled the 700-foot-deep Nisqually River canyon as La Grande, meaning "the large one." Later as part of a land development promotion, a Judge John McMurray, who owned a large tract that included a portion of the canyon, placed a sign along the roadway in 1904 which read: "Watch The Grand Canyon Grow." Thus, the townsite became known as La Grande, and the name was assigned to the hydroelectric plant opened at the site by the city of Tacoma in 1912.

Lake Ballinger. *See* Ballinger, Lake.

Lakebay (Pierce). Town and bay on the shore of Carr Inlet were named—by reversal of words—for adjacent Bay Lake.

Lake Chelan. *See* Chelan.

Lake Crescent. *See* Crescent, Lake.

Lake Cushman. *See* Cushman, Lake.

Lake Ozette. *See* Ozette, Lake.

Lake Sammamish. *See* Sammamish, Lake.

Lake Stevens. *See* Stevens, Lake.

Lake Sutherland. *See* Sutherland, Lake.

Lake Union. *See* Union, Lake.

Lakeview (Pierce). The community began in 1896 as a railroad station named for its proximity to a small lake.

Lake Washington. *See* Washington, Lake.

Lake Whatcom. *See* Whatcom, Lake.

Lakewood Center (Pierce). Centered by a planned shopping complex, the community derived its name from its location in a wooded residential area in the American-Gravelly Lakes district south of Tacoma.

Lamona, luh-MOH-nuh (Lincoln). Named for merchant J. H. Lamona, who opened a store in 1892.

Lamont (Whitman). Named for Daniel Lamont, vice president of the Northern Pacific Railroad.

Langley (Island). Town on the southeastern shore of Whidbey Island was platted in 1890 by Jacob Anthes and named for Seattle Judge J. W. Langley, a partner in Anthes' land development company.

Langley Point (Skagit). This southwestern point on Fidalgo Island was named for a pioneer settler who lived on the adjacent bay.

La Push, luh-POOSH (Clallam). An infusion of the French term *la bouche,* meaning "mouth," into the Chinook jargon, and descriptive of the town's position at the mouth of the Quillayute River on the Quillayute Indian Reservation.

Larson Air Force Base (Grant). Named in honor of Maj. Donald A. Larson, a World War II pilot from nearby Yakima, who was killed over Germany in 1944.

Latah, LAY-tah (Spokane). The community was first settled in 1870 as Alpha, but the name was changed in 1875 to coincide with that of nearby Latah Creek. The stream was originally called Hangman Creek because in 1858 Col. George Wright killed nearly 800 horses and hanged several Indians along its banks in retaliation for the Palouse warriors' defeat of Lt. Col. Edward J. Steptoe. The gruesome name was changed by the legislature to Latah Creek, an adaptation of the Indian name Lahtoo that described the "stream where little fish are caught."

Laurel (Klickitat). Named for the laurel bushes that grow profusely on the Camas Prairie.

Laurier, law-ree-AY (Ferry). Named in 1902 by the Great Northern Railroad for Canadian Premier Sir Wilfred Laurier.

Lawrence (Whatcom). Vaguely named to honor Laura Blankenship, daughter of the town's sawmill operator.

Lawton, Fort (King). Situated on Seattle's Magnolia Bluff, the U.S.

Army post was named in 1900 to honor Maj. Gen. Henry W. Lawton, who was killed in the Philippine Islands in 1899.

Leadbetter Point (Pacific). The southern tip of Willapa Harbor entrance honors Lt. Danville Leadbetter, one of the officers of the U.S. Coast Survey expedition of 1852.

Leadpoint (Stevens). Named for nearby Electric Point Lead Mine.

Leavenworth (Chelan). Original community of Icle became a Great Northern Railroad construction camp. Platted in 1893 by the railroad's "Captain" Charles F. Leavenworth, nephew of the founder of Leavenworth, Ks., the town adopted the family name.

Lebam, li-BAM (Pacific). J. W. Goodell created the town name by spelling his daughter Mabel's name backward.

Leland (Jefferson). Name was intended to honor Mrs. Laura E. Andrews, the first woman to settle in the valley, by coining a name from her initials, but the postal authorities spelled the name Leland instead of *Lea*land.

Lemolo, lee-MOH-loh (Kitsap). A Chinook jargon word meaning "wild" or "untamed." A French-Canadian addition to the trade language, meaning "a runaway Negro slave," derived from the French word *Le More,* which was converted to the present form by the Indians' inability to pronounce the letter *r.* It was used to describe anything or anybody untamed.

Lester (King). Established in the 1880s as Deans for Dean Sawmill Co., the town was renamed, *circa* 1891, for Lester Hansacker, a telegrapher who worked at the section house there during construction of the Northern Pacific Railroad.

Lewis, Fort (Pierce). Constructed in 1917 as Camp Lewis on land donated by Pierce County, and redesignated as a fort in 1927, the post is named for Capt. Meriwether Lewis of the Lewis and Clark Expedition.

Lewis County; 2,447 sq. mi.; 6th in size; seat: Chehalis. Named in honor of Capt. Meriwether Lewis of the Lewis and Clark Expedition of 1804–6 which spent from 11 October 1805 to 5 May 1806 in what are now the states of Washington and Oregon. Just as controversy exists as to who was the "real" leader of the historic expedition, so does the debate as to whether Lewis or Clark was the leader among Washington counties. Clark County is the oldest still existing unit of government in the state. Lewis, the second senior unit of government, is actually the oldest *county* in fact and in name. On 20 August 1845 the provisional legislature of the territory of Oregon created Vancouver District out of that portion of Oregon Territory north of the Columbia River. The following day the legislature created Lewis County out of the vast western portion of the Vancouver District (which then extended northward from the Columbia River to the "54–40" boundary in dispute with England). On 3 September 1849 the Oregon Territorial Legislature passed a law that read: "That the name of County of Vancouver be, and hereby is, changed to Clark." Thus, the change in terms from Vancouver District to Vancouver County gives belated, but added, support to those who contend that Clark is the oldest county. Yet Lewis supporters point out that the change from district to county is immaterial, what really counts is the fact that Lewis County was a separate entity while Clark needed a name change to come into existence. [*See* Clark County.]

Lewis River. The tributary of the Columbia River, rising in Skamania County and forming the border between Clark and Cowlitz counties, was named for A. Lee Lewis, who homesteaded near its mouth. [*See* Snake River.]

Liberty (Kittitas). Gold-mining community on Swauk Creek was originally called Meaghersville for early prospector Tommy Meagher. In 1892 miners changed the name of the boom town to fit Postmaster Gus Nelson's oft-repeated invitation "to feel at liberty to do what you want, this is really your place."

Liberty Bay (Kitsap). Despite pleas of Poulsbo residents, the state legislature in 1893 and 1899 humorously refused to change the official title of Dog Fish Bay to the more euphonic Liberty Bay, so the present name was adopted through general usage. The original name was a location tie in to the bay-shore plant Harry Drescott operated *circa* 1860 to render dogfish oil used to grease the logs that made up lumber camp skid roads.

Liberty Lake (Spokane). Lake and town are named for former Hudson's Bay Co. employee Etienne Eduard Laliberte, who, under the name Steve Liberty, homesteaded on the lake shore. Liberty and nearby Newman Lake both are named for French-Canadian farmers who anglicized the spelling of their surnames, worked for Hudson's Bay Co., and married daughters of Antoine La Plante, operator of the first Spokane River ferry at Irvin.

Lilliwaup, LIL-uh-wahp (Mason). Town, creek, falls, and bay on Hood Canal named with a Twana Indian word meaning "inlet."

Lincoln County; 2,300 sq. mi.; 7th in size; seat: Davenport. Created 24 November 1883 and named in honor of President Abraham Lincoln by the territorial legislature, which four days later named the adjacent county after Lincoln's political rival Stephen A. Douglas. Also abutting Lincoln County is Grant County, named for the Union's victorious general in the Civil War. The community of Lincoln was subsequently named as a geographic tie in to the county.

Lincoln Creek (Lewis). This small tributary of the Chehalis River was initially known by its Indian name Matchel, meaning "a place where edible-root camas plants grew in abundance." Frank M. Rhodes, an ardent Republican who homesteaded on the stream, officially renamed it after then President Abraham Lincoln in the presence of four other Centralia area pioneers.

Lind (Adams). Named in 1881 as the site of a Northern Pacific Railroad water tank and section house. Exact origin of the name has been lost, but the three most frequently cited sources, in order of probability, are: after a woman cook with the track-laying crew; for an early settler in the county; as a whimsical honor for singer Jenny Lind, the Swedish nightingale. The Scandinavian influence of the name's origin was heightened in 1888 by the Nielson brothers, who platted the town in such a manner that the initial letters of its street names spelled their surname.

Lindberg (Lewis). Named for Gustof Lindberg, Tacoma sawmill operator, whose mill and logging camp started the town.

Lion Gulch (Kittitas). Self-named by prospector Pat Lions.

Liplip Point (Jefferson). Wilkes named the southeastern point on Marrowstone Island with the Chinook jargon word for "boiling."

Lisabeula, LIZ-a-BYOO-luh (King). Community on the western shore of Vashon Island was named by Postmaster Butts for his daughters Eliza and Beulah by joining their names and dropping the first and last letters, respectively.

Littell (Lewis). Honors early settler Curtis R. Littell.

Little Boston (Kitsap). Port Gamble Indian Reservation derives its name from adjacent Boston Point, a point on Hood Canal titled by Wilkes but no longer found on maritime charts.

Littlerock (Thurston). Named by an early settler for a stepped boulder "shaped by nature for a perfect [horse] mounting stone."

Locke (Pend Oreille). Named for original landowner.

Lofall, LOH-fawl (Kitsap). Former Hood Canal ferry community was named in honor of early settler H. Lofall.

Long Beach (Pacific). Descriptive name for the 28-mile-long beach of hard-packed sand and for the summer resort community near its southern end. As a carry-over from Oregon Territorial days, the so-called Long Beach Peninsula is still officially designated by the federal government as North Beach Peninsula.

Longbranch (Pierce). Named for a town in New Jersey. Branch is an early Americanism for creek and is still used by southerners, who insist on "branch water" as the proper mix for bourbon.

Longmire (Pierce). Location of the administrative headquarters for Mt. Rainier National Park was named for James Longmire, who established an inn by the "medical springs" in 1883. Longmire was leader of the first wagon train to cross the Cascade Mountains from Walla Walla to Puget Sound country via Naches Pass in 1853. [*See* Rainier, Mt.]

Longview (Cowlitz). The first planned city in the Pacific Northwest, it is named for its founder R. A. Long, lumber baron, who founded the mill city in 1923. Because of its strategic location on a delta between the Cowlitz and Columbia rivers, it was the site of a Hudson's Bay Co. hide and fur warehouse in 1846. In 1849 two Americans, Jonathan Durbee and H. D. Huntington, established claims. In 1852 the resultant community, called Monticello, was host to a pioneer meeting (Monticello Convention) which asked that the U.S. Congress create the territory of Columbia out of the Oregon Territory area north of the Columbia River. On 10 February 1853 a bill to establish the Columbia Territory was amended to substitute the name of the first President in place of Columbia, and on 2 March 1853 President Millard Fillmore signed the bill creating the Washington Territory. In 1854 the new territorial legislature formed Cowlitz County, with Monticello as its seat. Floods in 1866–67 washed the town away, and the delta was reclaimed by swamps. [*See* Monticello.]

Loomis (Okanogan). Name honors J. A. Loomis, the town's first merchant.

Loon Lake (Stevens). The town was named after the adjacent lake, which was so named because it was an autumn habitat for loons.

Loop Loop (Okanogan). Old mining town's name derived from the French word *loup,* meaning "wolf," as Hudson's Bay trappers found the locale rich in furs. In current usage the name of the surrounding recreation area is reverting to the original spelling of "Loup Loup."

Lopez (San Juan). A small community located on, and named for, Lopez Island.

Lopez Island (San Juan). Eliza included the island in his Isla y Archipelago de San Juan. Wilkes named it for Commodore Isaac Chauncy, over-all commander of United States forces on the Great

Lakes during the War of 1812. Kellett, in redoing charts in 1857, assigned to the island the first name of Lopez Gonzales de Haro, reputed to be the sailing master in Eliza's command who actually discovered the San Juans. Another of his namesakes is Haro Strait that marks the western boundary of both San Juan County and the United States.

Loveland (Pierce). Named for early settlers in the area.

Lowden, LOW-duhn (Walla Walla). Named for early pioneer settler Francis M. Lowden, Sr., in 1899.

Lucerne, loo-SERN (Chelan). Resort community on Lake Chelan named in 1903 by a settler because the lake was reminiscent of her home in Switzerland.

Ludlow, Port. *See* Port Ludlow.

Lummi Island, LUHM-ee (Whatcom). Eliza called it Isla de Pacheco, a portion of the name of the viceroy of Mexico. Wilkes changed the name to McLoughlin Island to honor Dr. John McLoughlin, Hudson's Bay Co. factor at Fort Vancouver. In 1853 the U.S. Coast Survey adopted the present name "because inhabited by the tribe." The Indian name Lummi or Nuh-lummi is applied to other geographic features in the area: Lummi Bay between the island and the mainland's Lummi Indian Reservation, through which flows the Lummi River.

Lyle (Klickitat). Originally as a steamboat landing on the Columbia River and subsequently as a town, this site bore the name of its first settler.

Lyman (Skagit). Named in 1880 for B. L. Lyman, the first postmaster.

Lynden (Whatcom). Mrs. Phoebe N. Judson, first white woman in the northern portion of the county, named the town in 1870 after a favorite poem, "Hohenlinden" by Thomas Campbell, in which the first verse begins: "On Linden, when the sun was low. . . ." She substituted "y" for "i" because she believed it would then look as pretty as it sounded.

Lynnwood (Snohomish). The town was named by combining the first name of Lynn Oburn, wife of one of the promoters, with a suffix that noted its then-sylvan setting.

IOOI

Mabana, muh-BAN-nuh (Island). The name of the community on Camano Island was coined in 1912 to honor Mabel Anderson, daughter of early settler Nils Anderson, by combining the first syllables of her first and last names and adding an *a* for a more pleasant sound.

Mabton (Yakima). Purportedly named for Mabel Baker, daughter of Dr. Dorsey S. Baker, early eastern Washington railroad builder of Walla Walla.

McChord Air Force Base (Pierce). Municipal airport acquired by the War Department in 1938, the airfield is named for Col. William C. McChord of the army air corps, who was killed in a crash in 1937.

McCleary (Grays Harbor). Named in 1911 for Henry McCleary, president of the logging and mill company that served as the area's main industry.

McGlinn Island (Skagit). Small island in Skagit Bay near the south entrance of Swinomish Slough was named for John P. McGlinn, La Conner hotel operator, *circa* 1877.

McGowen (Pacific). Named for Patrick J. McGowen, who purchased 320 acres of old Catholic mission land grant in 1853 and established a salmon-packing plant. The area was once the site of the principal village of the Chinook Indians on the Columbia River.

Machias, muh-CHEYE-uhs (Snohomish). Platted and named in 1888 by L. W. Getchell for his home town in Maine.

McKenna (Pierce). Named for a former Wisconsin resident who established a sawmill at the townsite in 1906.

McMillan (Pierce). First known as Lime Kiln, the town was given its present name in 1891 by John S. McMillan when he officially platted the townsite around the offices of his lime company.

McMurray (Skagit). Town and lake named for an early settler.

McNary Dam (Benton). The Columbia River dam is named for Charles McNary, United States Senator from Oregon, who was instrumental in securing appropriations for its construction.

McNeil Island (Pierce). Named by Wilkes in honor of William Henry McNeill [*sic*], Boston-born captain of the Hudson's Bay Co. steamer *Beaver*. British Capt. R. N. Inskip in 1846 sought to change the name to Duntze Island after Capt. John A. Duntze of the British frigate *Fisgard,* but Kellett restored the original name in 1847. In 1869 the U.S. Corps of Engineers founded a marshal's jail on the island, and since 1909 it has served as a federal penitentiary. [*See* Anderson Island; Pilot Point.]

Mae (Grant). Named in 1907 to honor Mrs. Mae Shoemaker, the first postmistress.

Magnolia Beach (King). Community on Vashon Island was named by the Silas Look family for their home town of Magnolia, Iowa.

Magnolia Bluff (King). Northern promontory of Elliott Bay and a residential section of Seattle was named in 1856 by Capt. George Davidson of the U.S. Coast Survey, who mistook native madroña trees for magnolia trees.

Malaga, MAL-uh-guh (Chelan). Named by an early-day farmer and irrigation system promoter for his vineyards of Malaga grapes which, in turn, bear the name of the Spanish province where they originated.

Malden (Whitman). Named by H. R. Williams after a town of the same name in Massachusetts.

Malo, MAL-oh (Ferry). Name source unverified.

Malone (Grays Harbor). Former company town operated by the

Vance Lumber Co. and named by Joseph A. Vance for a community in New York.

Malott, muh-LAHT (Okanogan). Name honors pioneer settler W. G. Malott.

Maltby (Snohomish). Original name of Yew was changed to honor Robert Maltby, real estate operator who promoted the townsite.

Manchester (Kitsap). A lumber- and shingle-mill town established as Brooklyn in 1883, the town was renamed for the English city as early civic leaders envisioned it also becoming a major seaport.

Manette, muh-NET (Kitsap). Now a part of Bremerton, the once separate town was named by residents for the first steamer that stopped at the community's wharf.

Manitou Beach, MAN-i-toh (Kitsap). An Algonquin Indian word meaning "spirit" that under various spellings has been transferred from the Great Lakes area to a variety of geographic entities throughout North America.

Mansfield (Douglas). Named in 1905 by R. E. Darling for his home town in Ohio, which, in turn, honored Col. Jared Mansfield, surveyor-general of the United States.

Manson (Chelan). The Lake Chelan community was named in 1912 by the Lake Chelan Land Co. in honor of Seattleite Manson F. Backus, president of the firm.

Manzanita, MAN-zuh-NEE-tuh (Kitsap). The community on the western shore of Bainbridge Island derived its name from the manzanita shrub, a member of the heath family that includes arbutus, azalea, and rhododendron.

Maple Falls (Whatcom). Named by millowner George A. King for the falls on Maple Creek when he platted the townsite on his homestead.

Maple Valley (King). Named Vine Maple Valley by the first settlers in 1879 because of the maple trees growing along that portion of the Cedar River, the name was shortened by postal officials in 1888.

Marble (Stevens). Named for extensive deposits of marble in the area.

Marblemount (Skagit). Named for the marble in the mountains surrounding the town.

Marcellus, mahr-SEL-uhs (Adams). One of the 32 locations in the state named by H. R. Williams. A few short years after bestowing the name, Williams advised Prof. Edmond S. Meany of the University of Washington that he named it "after some person in the East. I cannot now recall who it was."

March Point (Skagit). Given the Massachusetts Indian name Sachem or "head chief" by Wilkes, the east cape of Fidalgo Bay was changed by popular usage to honor farmer Hiram A. March, who achieved acclaim for the cauliflower seed he raised there *circa* 1891.

Marcus (Stevens). Relocated north of its original site because of the backwater of Coulee Dam, the town is the oldest in the county and was named for Marcus Oppenheimer, first settler and merchant.

Marengo, muh-RENG-goh (Adams). Named by H. R. Williams after the battle of Marengo in Italy on 14 June 1800, in which Napoleon defeated the Austrians.

Marietta (Whatcom). Platted in 1883 by Solomon Allen, who adapted the town's title from his wife's and daughter's given name of Mary.

Marlin (Grant). The corporate name of the community is Krupp, as originally assigned to the railway station by the Great Northern Railroad. However, the name of the post office serving the town is Marlin, the surname of the first settler in the area.

Marmes Site, MAHRM-uhs (Whitman). Archeological dig on the Palouse River near its junction with the Snake has skulls and artifacts establishing prehistoric man's presence on the American continent 13,000 years ago. Marmes Man bears the name of Roland Marmes, owner of the property on which the rock shelter was found.

Marrowstone Island (Jefferson). Vancouver so named the island's northern cliff because it was composed of "marrow stone," a soft clay resembling Fuller's earth. Wilkes attempted to affix the name Craven Peninsula in honor of the expedition's Lt. Thomas T. Craven, but general usage extended Vancouver's title to the entire land mass, and Craven's name was relegated to a large rock off-shore.

Marshall (Spokane). Named for early settler William H. Marshall.

Maryhill (Klickitat). Originally known as Columbus, the community was renamed when railroad magnate Samuel Hill built a lavish estate there overlooking the Columbia River and named it Maryhill to honor his wife and daughter, whose names were Mary.

Marysville (Snohomish). J. P. Comeford, Indian agent at the Tulalip Reservation, bought the land in 1872 and in 1877 constructed a store and wharf on Ebey Slough. Among the first settlers were James Johnson and Thomas Lloyd, who suggested that the new community be named for their former home of Marysville, Calif.

Mason County; 967 sq. mi.; 30th in size; seat: Shelton. Established 13 March 1854 under the Indian name of Sawamish County. It was renamed on 3 January 1864 to honor Charles H. Mason, first secretary of Washington Territory and acting governor during the Indian Wars. The first county seat was Oakland on Oakland Bay. [*See* Shelton.]

Massacre Bay (San Juan). The bay in West Sound, Orcas Island, touches Victim Island, Skull Rock, Indian Point, and Haida Point, which are all named because explorers found evidence of battles between local and northern Indians.

Matia Island, MAY-shuh (San Juan). Called Isla de Mata, meaning "no protection," by Eliza.

Matlock (Mason). First called Mason, the town was renamed in the late 1890s by early settler James Hodgkinson for his home town in England.

Mats Mats Bay (Jefferson). A Clallam Indian term meaning "opened and closed" refers to high and low tides, which allowed or restricted entry to the bay via a shallow passage.

Mattawa, MAT-a-wuh (Grant). Named with an Indian word

meaning "Where is it?" the town is built on the old Priest Rapids townsite that was platted in 1909.

Maury Island, MAWR-ee (King). The peninsula on the southeastern sector of Vashon Island was erroneously charted as an island. It was called Maury's Island by Wilkes for the expedition's Lt. William L. Maury. [*See* Portage.]

Maxwelton (Island). Whidbey Island summer community named by the Mackie brothers for "the bonny braes of Scotland."

Mayfield (Lewis). Town on the Cowlitz River was named for early settler Wilt Mayfield.

Mazama, muh-ZAH-muh (Okanogan). Looking for a euphemism for the original name of Goat Creek (a stream flowing past the community from nearby Goat Mountain), the residents chose what they thought was the Greek synonym. Their definition was right, but their language was wrong, as the word *mazama* is Spanish for "mountain goat."

Mead (Spokane). Named by James Berridge in honor of Civil War Gen. George Gordon Meade of the Union Army.

Meadowdale (Snohomish). Named by Robert Maltby in 1904 because he envisioned that "cleaned up and into grass it would be one vast meadow."

Medical Lake (Spokane). The town was named by early settlers for the lake. The Indians believed that the lake's waters would cure rheumatism.

Medina, me-DEYE-nuh (King). A Seattle suburban community on the eastern shore of Lake Washington was named in 1892 by Mrs. S. A. Belote for the Arabian holy city of Medina, where Mohammed is buried.

Megler (Pacific). The town was named for Joseph G. Megler, operator of a Columbia River fish cannery and a frequent member of the state legislature.

Memaloos Island, MEM-a-loos (Klickitat). This Columbia River island used by the Klickitat Indians as a cemetery was called Sepulchre Island by Lewis and Clark, who found 13 burial huts on it. A monument on the small island marks the grave of Vic Trevett, pioneer river man who requested interment there. The Indian word *memaloose* means "dead."

Menlo (Pacific). Northern Pacific construction crews selected Preston as the name of a station on the Willapa Harbor branch line. It was rejected as a duplication of another station's name, so the crew borrowed the sign "Menlo Park" from a real estate development down track, broke off the Park portion, and rechristened Preston as Menlo.

Mercer Island (King). The island and, hence, the community thereon were named for Judge Thomas Mercer, captain of a wagon train that arrived in Seattle in 1853, and the man who named Lake Washington and Lake Union. The judge was the elder brother of Asa Shinn Mercer, first president of the University of Washington, who brought the Mercer Girls contingent of husband-seekers to Seattle from the east coast.

Mesa, MEE-suh (Franklin). The town name is a misnomer in two respects. Its origin is the Spanish word *mesa* (pronounced MAY-suh), meaning "table land." Not only is the pronunciation altered locally, but the town is situated on rather low flat land surrounded by hills rather than on a steep-walled plateau.

Metaline Falls, MET-uh-leen (Pend Oreille). Because the surrounding area was mineral-rich, miners of the mid-1800s affixed the name Metaline to the cascades in the Pend Oreille [Clark Fork] River. The towns of Metaline Falls and Metaline both derive their names from proximity to the falls.

Methow, MET-how (Okanogan). Town, valley, and river derive their name from the name of the Indian tribe that originally occupied the pie-shaped sector formed by the Columbia River and Lake Chelan. The Indian name for the river was Buttlemuleemauch, meaning "salmon falls river."

Meydenbauer Bay, MAY-den-bower (King). The exclusive residential district on the eastern shore of Lake Washington near Bellevue was named for pioneer settler William Meydenbauer.

Mica, MEYE-kuh (Spokane). Both the town and Mica Peak were named for deposits of the mineral mica found in the area by early miners.

Midland (Pierce). So named because it was the midway station on the Tacoma-Puyallup electric rail line of the 1890s.

Midway (King). So named because it is half-way between Seattle and Tacoma on Route 99.

Migley, Point (Whatcom). William Migley, one of the gunners on the Wilkes Expedition, was the name source for the northern tip of Lummi Island.

Milan, mil-AN (Spokane). Named for Milan, Italy, home town of one of the construction workers on the Great Northern Railroad crew that established the railroad station in 1890.

Millwood (Spokane). Initially an electric railway station named Woodard for Seth Woodard, who settled in the Spokane Valley in 1883, the city was given its present name with the advent of a sawmill in 1910.

Milton (Pierce). A sawmill site initially, the city's present name is a contraction of the original name of Milltown.

Mineral (Lewis). Town on the lake of the same name. The area was named for its rich ore deposits, particularly red realgar from which arsenic is extracted.

Minnehaha, MIN-ee-haw-haw (Clark). A Sioux Indian word meaning "water falls" but romantically translated as "laughing water" was the name of the heroine in Henry Wadsworth Longfellow's "Song of Hiawatha." In addition to its native site in Minnesota, the name appears in such geographically diverse areas as South Dakota, West Virginia, and Washington.

Mission Beach (Snohomish). Small resort community on the southern shore of Tulalip Bay named for a Catholic mission and Indian cemetery established in the area in 1858. [*See* Tulalip.]

Moclips, MOH-klips (Grays Harbor). A Quinault Indian word describing a place where maidens were sent to undergo puberty rites.

Mohler (Lincoln). Renamed from Moroco to honor Morgan Mohler, a mail-stage driver on the Sprague run.

Molson (Okanogan). Named for Canadian businessman John W. Molson, who had mining interests in the area but never set foot on any of his Molson holdings.

Monitor (Chelan). Originally called Brown's Flat after Reuben A. Brown, who settled there in 1884. With establishment of the post office in 1902, residents voted in favor of the suggestion of George T. Richardson to change the town's name to commemorate the Civil War victory of the Union's iron-clad *Monitor* over the Confederate's armor-plated *Merrimac*.

Monohon, MAH-nuh-han (King). Misspelled tribute to early settler Martin Monohan, who homesteaded the townsite in 1877.

Monroe (Snohomish). Community was established in 1878 as Park Place by Salem Wood. In 1890 John Vanasdlen opened a post office in his store there, but called it Monroe when postal authorities rejected the town's original name. The Great Northern Railroad laid track a mile away, so Vanasdlen helped plat a new townsite called Tye. The railroad selected Wales as the name of its station there. So Vanasdlen moved the Monroe post office from Park Place to Tye-Wales, and railroad, postal, and civic officials agreed upon the name Monroe—a name with no known reason for its initial selection.

Monse, MAWNZ (Okanogan). Original name of Swansea was changed on 24 October 1916 to honor Mons, Belgium, where the British fought the first engagement of World War I on 23 August 1914.

Montborne, MAHNT-bern (Skagit). Settled in 1884 by Dr. N. P. Montborne of Mount Vernon and erroneously listed as Mount Bourne on some early maps.

Monte Cristo, mahnt-ee-KRIS-toh (Snohomish). Once linked to Everett by railroad, this ghost town is the center of a mining district rich in gold, silver, copper, and galena. It was named on 4

July 1889 by prospector Frank W. Peabody, who exclaimed to his partner Joseph Pearsell, "It's rich as the Count of Monte Cristo." The town's main street was named Dumas for Alexander Dumas, creator of the Count of Monte Cristo and Peabody's favorite author.

Montesano, mahn-tuh-SAY-noh (Grays Harbor). Established as Scammon after J. L. Scammons, an 1852 donation land claim settler on whose land the county seat town is situated. His wife, a devoutly religious woman, requested that the town be renamed Mount Zion. The present name is a more pleasant sounding compromise with much the same meaning.

Monticello, MAHN-tuh-sel-oh (Cowlitz). Named in 1849 for President Thomas Jefferson's home. The long-gone town was the site of a pioneer convention in 1852 that petitioned Congress for the creation of the Columbia (Washington) Territory out of the northern portion of the Oregon Territory. The number of white settlers in the area north of the Columbia River (including Idaho and parts of Montana and Wyoming) was approximately 4,000 at that time. [*See* Longview.]

Mora Beach, MOR-uh (Clallam). Both Mora on the Quillayute River and Mora Beach were named by K. O. Erickson after his home town in Sweden. The first postmaster had named the community Boston, but misdirection of mail to Massachusetts caused Erickson to rename the community when he took over the post office.

Moran State Park (San Juan). The site of Mt. Constitution on Orcas Island is named for Robert Moran, millionaire shipbuilder and former mayor of Seattle. Moran donated the park land to the state in 1921 and also built plush Rosario on East Sound as his private estate.

Morton (Lewis). Named in honor of Vermont Republican Levi P. Morton, who was vice president of the United States in 1889, the year Washington was granted statehood.

Moses Coulee (Douglas). Carved out by an Ice Age glacier, the coulee is named for an Indian chief whose band wintered at the bottom of the cliff-sided valley near Douglas Canyon.

Moses Lake (Grant). The lake was named for Chief Moses, whose tribe camped on the lake shore. The settlement of Neppel was re-named Moseslake upon establishment of a post office in 1906 and subsequently altered to its present form to coincide with the lake name.

Mossyrock (Lewis). An early trading post on the Cowlitz River was named Mossy Rock in 1852 after a 200-foot-high moss-covered rock at the east end of Klickitat Prairie. The Indians originally called the area Coulph.

Mt. Adams. *See* Adams, Mt.

Mt. Baker. *See* Baker, Mt.

Mt. Booker. *See* Booker, Mt.

Mt. Chatham. *See* Chatham, Mt.

Mt. Constance. *See* Constance, Mt.

Mt. Constitution. *See* Constitution, Mt.

Mt. Ellinor. *See* Ellinor, Mt.

Mt. Olympus. *See* Olympus, Mt.

Mt. Pickett. *See* Pickett, Mt.

Mt. Rainier. *See* Rainier, Mt.

Mt. St. Helens. *See* St. Helens, Mt.

Mt. Shuksan. *See* Shuksan, Mt.

Mt. Si. *See* Si, Mt.

Mount Vernon (Skagit). The county seat city established as a fur-trading post on the Skagit River was named after George Washington's Potomac River estate by E. C. English and Harrison Clothier in 1877. The Washington estate, willed to the first President by his brother Lewis, was named in honor of Adm. Edward Vernon of the British Navy.

Mowich Lake, MOH-ich (Pierce). The largest lake in Mt. Rainier National Park bears an Indian name meaning "deer," which has been extended to a glacier and a stream.

Moxee City, MAHK-see (Yakima). First settlers adopted the Indian word for "whirlwinds" as the name of their town as small dust spirals prevailed in the area.

Mukilteo, MUHK-il-TEE-oh (Snohomish). Originally known as Point Elliott, the town was founded by J. D. Fowler and Morris H. Frost, partners in a store. When Fowler became postmaster in 1862 he adopted as its name a variation of the Indian name Muckl-te-o, meaning "good camping ground." [*See* Elliot Point.]

Murray, Camp (Pierce). The headquarters of the Washington State National Guard derives its name from a railroad station at its site, which, in turn, was named for a nearby marshy creek that carries the name of an area pioneer, I. G. Murray.

Mutiny Bay (Island). Small bay on the southwestern shore of Whidbey Island was so charted by the U.S. Coast Survey in 1855 without explanation of the reason for the name selection.

---

n

Naches, na-CHEEZ (Yakima). An Indian name for a pass through the Cascade Range has also been given to several other geographic points: town, valley, river, etc. The Indian word *nahchess* means "plenty of water."

Nagrom, NAG-room (King). Small community named in 1911 for E. C. Morgan, president of a mill company located at the railroad stop, by spelling his name backward.

Nahcotta, NAH-KAH-tuh (Pacific). Named in the 1880s by early settler John P. Paul for a local Indian chief.

Napavine, NA-puh-veyen (Lewis). Name derived in 1883 by Scots immigrant James Urquart from the Indian word *napavoon,* meaning "small prairie."

Narrows, The (Pierce). Originally called Narrows by Wilkes, the name of the four-mile-long, one-mile-wide passageway into lower Puget Sound was formalized as The Narrows by Kellett on British Admiralty charts.

Naselle, nay-SEL (Pacific). Both the town and river originally carried the name Nasel, after the Nasal Indians, a branch of the Chinook tribe, who resided in the area.

Neah Bay, NEE-uh (Clallam). The harbor's name is derived from the Clallam Indian word *neeah,* which was their nasal pronunciation of the name Dee-ah, chief of the Makah tribe that lived in the area. Situated east of Cape Flattery on the Strait of Juan de Fuca, it was named Bahía de Núñez Gaono in 1790 by the Spanish. American fur traders subsequently called it Poverty Bay, and in 1841 Wilkes renamed it Scarborough Harbour in honor of Capt. James Scarborough of the Hudson's Bay Co. In 1847 Kellett recharted the place under its present name. The community of Neah Bay at Cape Flattery is the focal point of the Makah Indian Reservation, southernmost branch of the Nootka Tribe of British Columbia. The name Makah means "cape people." [*See* Alava, Cape; Ozette Lake; Tatoosh Island.]

Neilton (Grays Harbor). Originally named Jonesville after Neil A. Jones, the town adopted its patron's given name in the early 1920s when the post office was secured, as the former name was found to be duplicated several times throughout the nation.

Nespelem, nez-PEE-luhm (Okanogan). The Indian name Nespilim, meaning "flat land," was used by the natives to refer to the tribe, river, and valley. Near the town on the Colville Indian Reservation is the grave of Chief Joseph, leader of the Nez Perce in the war of 1877.

Newaukum, noo-AW-kuhm (Lewis). Name of a tributary of the Chehalis River and a small community is from the Indian word *nawakum,* meaning "gently flowing water."

New Castle (King). Community name adopted from that of the

Newcastle Coal Mine operated in the area by the Whitworth family of Seattle in 1869. The mine was named with reference to the English coal-mining center of Newcastle.

Newhalem, NOO-hay-luhm (Whatcom). Seattle City Light's gateway town to its Skagit River dams—Gorge, Diablo, and Ross—was named for Newhalem Creek, a tributary that joins the Skagit River at the community site. The name is a corruption of the Indian word *ne-whalem,* meaning "goat snare." [*See* Diablo.]

Newman Lake (Spokane). The lake was named for a French-Canadian settler who farmed the area. The nearby town was originally named Moab, but the name was changed in the late 1920s to avoid confusion with a similarly named town in Utah. [*See* Liberty Lake.]

Newport (Pend Oreille). County seat town received its name from construction of a landing dock to accommodate the first steamboat on the Pend Oreille River in 1890.

Nighthawk (Okanogan). Named for a nearby mine which, in turn, was named for the mottled brown relative of the whippoorwill prevalent in the area.

Nine Mile Falls (Spokane). The Spokane River community was originally called Helen but was changed to its present name in 1912 to record its location at the site of the hydroelectric dam nine miles downstream from the city of Spokane.

Nisqually, nis-KWAHL-ee (Thurston). Name of the town, river, valley, flats, glacier, bluff, and other geographic points is that of the Indian tribe of the area. The name derives from French explorers, who called the Indians *nez quarré,* meaning "square nose," and was altered by the natives' inability to pronounce the letter *r*. The first white settlement on Puget Sound, Hudson's Bay's Fort Nisqually built in 1833, was situated near the mouth of the Nisqually River. [*See* Du Pont, Ketron Island.]

Nisson, NIS-suhn (Grays Harbor). An adaptation of Nilson, the name of an early-day logger in the area.

Nodule Point, NOHD-yool (Jefferson). So named by Vancouver for the peculiarly shaped geological formations on the southeastern shore of Marrowstone Island. Wilkes renamed it Point Ariel for one of his small boats, but in 1868 the U.S. Coast Survey reconfirmed the original title.

Nooksack, NOOK-sak (Whatcom). River and town preserve the name of the Nooksack Indians or "mountain men" living in the area. The tribe was originally a part of the Squawmish tribe of British Columbia.

Nordland (Jefferson). Town on Marrowstone Island was named *circa* 1890 for Peter Nordby, who owned the townsite land.

Norman (Snohomish). Named for P. O. Norman, early settler in the Stillaguamish River Valley.

Normandy Park (King). Developed in the late 1920s by the Seattle-Tacoma Land Co., which so named the community in keeping with promotional plans to restrict residence construction to French Normandy architecture.

North Bend (King). So named because it is located on a sharp north bend in the south fork of the Snoqualmie River. The town was platted in 1889 by William H. Taylor as Snoqualmie, but lost that title through general usage to a community closer to the Snoqualmie Falls. It was called Mountain View and South Fork before the present name was adopted.

North Bluff (Island). Bluff at the north entrance to Holmes Harbor on Whidbey Island was named by Wilkes, not for its northerly position, but for James North, master of the expedition's *Vincennes*.

North Bonneville, BAHN-uh-vil (Skamania). The area post office was established in 1851 and repeatedly changed names—Hamilton, Moffett Springs, Table Rock, Wacomac (after an Indian chief), and Moffetts—with changes in postmasters. The dwindling community, which enjoyed resurgence with construction of the Bonneville Dam, changed its name to capitalize on its location at the northern side of the dam. [*See* Bonneville Dam.]

Northport (Stevens). The title appropriately describes the community's location as the northernmost United States town on the

Columbia River. Platted in 1892 as a smelter site, the town was a major ore and building-stone shipping point on the Spokane Falls and Northern Railroad.

Northrup (King). Named for one-time state land commissioner, George Northrup.

Norwegian Point (Kitsap). Site of resort town of Hansville was so named because of early settlement by individuals of Norwegian extraction.

Novelty (King). Named in 1871 by first settler George Boyce for his home town in Missouri, whose name, in turn, had originated from a conscious effort to choose a "novel" title.

Oakesdale (Whitman). Named by the Northern Pacific Land Co. in honor of Thomas F. Oakes, vice president of the Northern Pacific Railroad in 1886.

Oak Harbor (Island). The second oldest settlement in Island County, the town was named because of the large number of native oak trees in the area of the harbor.

Oakland Bay (Mason). Situated at the head of Hammersley Inlet, it was named in 1852 by pioneer settler William T. Morrow for a scattering of oak trees in the area. Oakland community on the bay's western shore was the original county seat. [*See* Shelton.]

Oakville (Grays Harbor). Named for scrub oak trees in the area, the town, which is situated on an old Indian campground, enjoyed a short-lived boom in the early 1900s as a "boarding house" community for railroad construction workers and was subsequently a major collection point for cascara bark.

Obstruction Island (San Juan). So named by Wilkes because it virtually blocks the waterway between Orcas and Blakely islands.

Ocean City (Grays Harbor). Summer community named because of its position on the Pacific Ocean beach.

Ocean Park (Pacific). Established in 1883 as a Methodist Church resort community patterned after Ocean Grove Church Camp on the New Jersey coast.

Ocean Shores (Grays Harbor). A beach community on the sandy peninsula north of the entrance to Grays Harbor that was promoted in the 1950s as a major tourist center and year-around resort town.

Ocosta, oh-KAHS-tuh (Grays Harbor). Name was coined from the Spanish word *costa,* meaning "coast," prefixed with an "o" for euphony in 1891 by the company that developed the townsite.

Odessa (Lincoln). Named in 1892 after the Russian wheat-growing and -shipping city on the Black Sea because of Russian immigrants who were developing wheat ranches in the area of the Great Northern Railroad station.

Offut, AHF-uht (Thurston). Lake and community bear the family name of two brothers, Levi James and Milford Offut, who settled in the area in the late 1850s.

Ohanapecosh Hot Springs, oh-HAN-up-pee-kahsh (Lewis). Summer resort community and nearby river bear as their names an Indian term that literally translates as "Oh, look!" as in looking at something beautiful.

Ohop, OH-hahp (Pierce). The name of a small community, a lake, and a creek is derived from the Indian word *owhap,* meaning "water rushing out," affixed to the stream by the surveyor-general of Washington Territory in 1857.

Okanogan, oh-kuh-NAH-guhn (Okanogan). The county seat was established in 1888 as Alma, but because of the proliferation of that name in the U.S. Postal Guide city officials—in quest for something uncommon and distinctive—christened it Pogue for Dr. J. T.

Pogue, orchardist and former state senator. Residents found the name too different, and in 1907 it was given the present title.

Okanogan County; 5,294 sq. mi.; 1st in size; seat: Okanogan. Named for an Indian tribe, the county was organized by the territorial legislature on 2 February 1888. The name is derived from the Indian word *okanagen,* meaning "rendezvous," and was applied originally to the river's head at Osoyoos Lake where Canadian and United States Indians gathered annually to catch and cure fish, to trade, and to hold potlatches. The name was gradually applied to the river and to the tribe that lived along its banks.

Olalla, oh-LAL-uh (Kitsap). Settled by Scandinavian strawberry growers, the area was called *olallie,* meaning "many berries," by migratory Indians, and a phonetic adaptation of the Chinook jargon word was adopted as the town name.

Olequa, OH-luh-kwah (Cowlitz). Creek and rural community are known by the Indian name, meaning "where salmon come to spawn."

Olga (San Juan). The Orcas Island town was named after the mother of its first postmaster.

Olympia (Thurston). To the Indians it was Stitchas, meaning "bear's place." In 1846 the whites combined the surnames of its first two settlers—Edmund Sylvester and L. L. Smith—and called it Smithter, which gave way to the more conventional Smithfield. The seat of Thurston County and the capital of the state was renamed for the Olympic Mountains at the suggestion of United States customs collector Isaac N. Ebey, who had as a book in his library Olympia Fulvia Morata's *Critical Observation on Homer.* [*See* Ebey, Fort.]

Olympic Mountains. The coastal mountains lying between Grays Harbor and the Strait of Juan de Fuca, the Pacific Ocean and Hood Canal; the Olympic National Park which evolved from the national forest created by President Theodore Roosevelt in 1907; and the Olympic Peninsula on which they are located, derive their name from the range's highest peak, Mt. Olympus, 7,954 feet.

Olympus, Mt. (Jefferson). The highest peak in the Olympics was the first geographical feature in the present state of Washington to be named by a white man. It was sighted in 1774 by Spanish explorer Juan Perez who named it El Cerro de la Santa Rosalia, "The Mountain of Saint Rosalia." On 4 July 1778 British Capt. John Meares gave it the ancient Greek name for the "Home of the Gods."

Omak, OH-mak (Okanogan). The largest city in the county, it was platted in 1907 in an alfalfa field paralleling the Okanogan River. It derived its name from a nearby lake the Indians called *omache,* meaning "good medicine," as the water was believed to have medicinal qualities.

Onalaska, ohn-uh-LAS-kuh (Lewis). A Wisconsin town was named by a resident impressed by Thomas Campbell's poem, "Pleasures of Hope," which mentions the Alaska village (now spelled Unalaska). A resident of the Wisconsin town founded the Carlisle Lumber Co. and successively extended operations to Arkansas, Texas, and, finally in 1914, to Washington—and in each state duplicated the Aleut Indian name of his former home.

O'Neal Island (San Juan). Small island off the northeastern coast of San Juan Island was named by Wilkes for a naval hero as part of his scheme to convert the San Juan Islands to the Navy Archipelago.

Opportunity (Spokane). Area was developed by the Modern Irrigation and Land Co. in 1905, with real estate promoters conducting a public contest for a suitable name for the community. The winner was Miss Laura Kelsey; the prize was $10.00.

Orcas, OR-kuhs (San Juan). Ferry dock community situated on and named for Orcas Island.

Orcas Island (San Juan). This name is another of the many shortened versions of the name of the viceroy of Mexico, sponsor of Eliza's voyage through the San Juans in 1791. Actually, the Spanish did not name the island, but merely included it as part of the archipelago. It was Kellett who assigned the name, an adaptation of Horcasitas, when he reorganized the official British Admiralty charts in 1847. All the American, naval-hero names that Wilkes assigned in 1841—Hull Island for Orcas Island, Ironsides Inlet for East Sound, Guerrier Bay for West Sound—have disappeared except Mt. Constitution. It was Wilkes's identification pattern to link the name of a naval hero with that of his ship by close geographic proximity. For example, Commodore Isaac Hull won fame as commander of the United States frigate *Constitution* (Old Ironsides) when it captured the British warship *Guerrière* in the War of 1812. [*See* San Juan Islands.]

Orchards (Clark). Planting of extensive prune orchards in 1909 prompted the change of the community name from Fourth Plain.

Oregon, OR-ee-guhn. Mystery shrouds the name of the "Oregon Country" which initially encompassed the present states of Oregon, Washington, and Idaho as well as portions of Montana and Wyoming. The first recorded use of the word was by British army officer, Maj. Robert Rogers, who mentioned Ourigan in a 1765 proposal for exploration of the country west of the Great Lakes. The expedition was denied, but the major was assigned as commandant of the frontier post at Mackinac, Mich. The following year Jonathan Carver of Weymouth, Mass., outfitted at the fort for a journey to the upper Mississippi Valley. In 1778 he published a book, *Three Years' Travels Throughout the Interior Parts of North America . . . ,* in which he mentioned "the River Oregon, or the River of the West, that falls into the Pacific Ocean at the Straits of Anian." Vancouver, Gray, and Lewis and Clark seemed unaware of the name as they neither mentioned nor used it during their sojourns in the region. However, it gradually worked its way into the literature as the over-all title for the Pacific Northwest, largely because of its use by the poet William C. Bryant in his "Thanatopsis," published in 1817. While its source is unclear, experts tend to agree that the term originated in the area of the Mississippi River as an adaptation of a French, Spanish, or Indian word.

Orient (Ferry). Originally called Morgan, it was renamed in 1901 for the Orient Gold Mine on the outskirts of the town.

Orillia, or-IL-eeuh (King). Named in 1887 by Malcolm McDougall after his lake-front home town in Canada. The name is from the Spanish *orilla,* meaning "lesser shore," and was first applied in Ontario, Canada, by a former British officer who gave two adjacent towns Spanish names appropriate to their setting: Oro, facing large Lake Simcoe, and Orillia, facing the smaller Lake Conchicking.

Orin, OR-in (Stevens). Rural community and former post office named for Orin S. Winslow.

Orondo, or-AHN-doh (Douglas). Named by Dr. J. B. Smith, first settler, in response to the postal rule to select an unduplicated name for a new post office. Orondo was chief of the legendary people who operated copper mines in the Lake Superior region in pre-Indian times. Purportedly the mythical miners were emigrants from the lost continent of Atlantis, who escaped just prior to its sinking.

Oroville (Okanogan). The gold-mining town was given the Spanish name *oro* or "gold" in 1890. The "ville" was added in 1893 to avoid confusion with the town of Oso in Snohomish County.

Orting (Pierce). Since 1891, site of the state soldiers' home. The town was originally called Carbon, but there was confusion with nearby Carbonado. The mix-up was ended in 1878 when the railroad arrived and suggested a new name—an Indian word *orting,* purported to mean "prairie village."

Oso, OH-soh (Snohomish). Originally named Allen in honor of United States Senator John B. Allen, the town was renamed when Allyn, Mason County, was established. The new name is Spanish for "bear" and was suggested by J. B. Britizius after a town in Texas.

Osoyoos Lake, oh-SOO-yuhs (Okanogan). The name for the large lake through which the Okanogan River flows at the United States–Canadian boundary is from the Indian word *sooyos,* meaning "narrows." The origin of the prefix *O* is unknown.

Ostrander (Cowlitz). Community and creek named for Dr. Nathaniel Ostrander, pioneer homesteader.

Ostrich Bay (Kitsap). Wilkes so named the southern arm of Dye Inlet because its outline resembled the giant bird. Because of its odd shape, the original bay has been divided into two separately named units, Ostrich Bay and Oyster Bay.

Othello (Adams). Named by H. R. Williams after Shakespeare's play. Three other nearby stations named by Williams were: Corfu for an island off the coast of Greece, Smyrna for a gulf in the Aegean Sea, and Jericho after the Biblical town in Palestine.

Otis Orchards (Spokane). Originally a railroad flag station called Otis after an early settler, the name was amended in 1908 with establishment of a post office to tie in to the area's image as a fruit-growing center.

Outlook (Yakima). When a telephone toll station was installed to connect the distant cattle ranch of E. W. Dooley with his Yakima residence, company officials rejected his surname for the identifying call code. The ranch's view of a wide expanse of sagebrush led to selection of the word Outlook, a name adopted by the railroad for its siding station when tracks were subsequently laid eight miles to the south.

Ovington (Clallam). Name honors E. J. Ovington who built a resort on Lake Crescent in 1905.

Oyhut, OI-huht (Grays Harbor). Sometimes misspelled "Oyehut" on maps and road signs, the name stems from the Chinook Jargon word *ooahut* meaning "trail" or "passage to."

Oysterville (Pacific). Once the county seat, the community on the western shore of Willapa Bay was settled and named—for oyster harvesting—in 1854 by Isaac Alonzo Clark and R. H. Espey.

Ozette, Lake, oh-ZET (Clallam). The name for the lake and adjacent Indian Reservation is derived from that of the southernmost Makah settlement, called Ho-selth. [*See* Alava, Cape; Neah Bay; Tatoosh Island.]

P

Pacific (King). The town was platted in 1906 as a "real estate addition to Seattle," its name selected to extol the peaceful environs of the land development.

Pacific Beach (Grays Harbor). Descriptive of the town's setting on the Pacific Ocean shore.

Pacific County; 925 sq. mi.; 29th in size; seat: South Bend. Created by the Oregon Territorial Legislature on 4 February 1851 and named for its ocean boundary.

Packwood (Lewis). Town and lake honor William Packwood, who explored the Oregon Territory in 1844 and settled on the Nisqually Flats in 1887.

Paha, PAH-hah (Adams). An Indian word meaning "big water," for the spring located at the former townsite.

Paine Field (Snohomish). The airport name was affixed by the U.S. Army Air Force just prior to the outbreak of World War II to honor the memory of early-day mail pilot Topliff Paine, scion of a pioneer Everett family.

Palisades (Douglas). Named in 1906 by Seattleite George A. Virtue because of the sharp-pointed, fortress-like appearance of basaltic rocks characteristic of Moses Coulee.

Palix River, PAY-licks (Pacific). The short river that flows into

Willapa Bay derived its name from the Chehalis Indian language word *copalux,* meaning "slough covered with trees."

Palmer (King). Community named after the first agent in charge of the railway station.

Palouse, puh-LOOS (Whitman). City, river, falls, and a large general area of wheat country in the southeastern part of the state all bear the name of an Indian tribe that inhabited the region. Scholars speculate that the original Indian name for the tribe—Palus, Palloatpallah, or Pelusha—was converted by the French-Canadian *voyageurs* of the fur companies to the more familiar French word *pelouse,* meaning "ground covered with short, thick grass." The result of the transliteration was *palouse,* a term that aptly fitted the country.

Paradise Inn (Pierce). Paradise Valley was named for its beauty by Mrs. James Longmire, whose husband extensively explored the Mt. Rainier area. The name has been extended to a river, a glacier, and a resort inn.

Park (Whatcom). Community on Lake Whatcom was named for early settler Charles Park.

Parker (Yakima). Name honors early settler William Parker.

Parkland (Pierce). The Tacoma suburb came into being as a result of the establishment of Pacific Lutheran Academy in 1890. In 1894 the townsite was platted around the school's campus under its present name.

Partridge, Point (Island). Named by Vancouver to honor a family named Partridge into which his brother John had married.

Pasco, PAS-koh (Franklin). County seat town received its name from railroad surveyors who, suffering from the flatland heat, named it in contrast after Cerro de Pasco, a mining town in the cool atmosphere of a 15,000-foot-high mountain in Peru. [*See* Tri-Cities.]

Pass Island (Skagit). Small island that forms the center support for the Deception Pass Bridge and joins Whidbey Island to the mainland via Fidalgo Island.

Pataha City, puh-TAH-huh (Garfield). The name is a Nez Perce word meaning "brush" and was the Indian's descriptive term for the site, as the adjacent creek was bordered with brush. Settled in 1861 by James Bowers, the site was platted as a town in 1882 by former stagecoach driver Angevine June "Vine" Favor, and was known briefly as Waterstown and Favorsburg.

Pateros, puh-TAIR-uhs (Okanogan). Initially known as Nosler's Hotel, the town was established as Nera on 7 December 1895, and changed to Ives Landing four months later. Renamed in 1900 by former army Lt. Charles E. Nosler for a town of the same name in the Philippine Islands near which he had campaigned during the Spanish-American War.

Paterson (Benton). Established as Scott in 1890 and renamed for pioneer settler and first postmaster Henry Paterson in 1901.

Patos Island, PA-tohs (San Juan). Translated from the Spanish; *pato* means "duck." The name was assigned by Cmdr. Dionisio Alcalá Galiano of the *Sutil* and Capt. Cayetano Valdés of the *Mexicana* in 1792.

Peales Passage (Mason). Waterway separating Squaxin and Hart- stene islands was named by Wilkes for T. R. Peale, one of the expedition's naturalists.

Pearson (Kitsap). Family name of early settlers in the area.

Pe Ell, pee-EL (Lewis). The town was platted in the 1880s by Omar Mauermann on his homestead on Pe Ell Prairie. The prairie's name was adopted as the town name in the belief that it was an Indian word, but subsequent research disclosed that it was the natives' mispronunciation of the French name Pierre. French- Canadian Pierre Charles, a former Hudson's Bay Co. employee, had pastured horses in the region in the 1850s, and the Indians called the prairie after him. Their usual slurring of the letter *r* to an *l* sound resulted in Pierre becoming Pe Ell. [*See* Boistfort.]

Pend Oreille County, PAHN-do-RAY; 1,406 sq. mi.; 26th in size; seat: Newport. Youngest of the state's 39 counties, it was created by the legislature on 1 March 1911 and given the tribal name of

Indians who originally inhabited the area along the northern portion of the Washington-Idaho border. Because they wore shell ornaments in their ears, the natives were called "ear bobs" by early French fur traders, who used a colloquial version of the French term *pendant d'oreille*.

Pend Oreille River. It is actually a three-state, two-country river that rises in the Rocky Mountains of the United States and ends in Canada. It begins as the Clark Fork River (so named by the Lewis and Clark Expedition) near Butte, Mont., travels 300 miles to Idaho's Lake Pend Oreille, and emerges 35 miles further west as the Pend Oreille River. It flows into Washington State, turns north through Pend Oreille County, and crosses the border into British Columbia, where it joins the Columbia River.

Penn Cove (Island). Harbor at Coupeville named by Vancouver "in honor of a particular friend," the grandson of William Penn.

Peshastin, peh-SHAS-tin (Chelan). Town name is the Indian word meaning "wide-bottom canyon."

Pickering Passage (Mason). Waterway between the mainland and Hartstene Island was named by Wilkes for one of the expedition's naturalists, Charles Pickering.

Pickett, Mt. (San Juan). The Orcas Island mountain bears the name of Gen. George E. Pickett, famed Confederate general who led the charge at Gettysburg in 1863, in honor of his service as a U.S. Army captain in the San Juan boundary dispute (Pig War) in 1859.

Pierce County; 1,676 sq. mi.; 23rd in size; seat: Tacoma. Named in honor of Franklin Pierce, who was President-elect when the Oregon Territorial Legislature established the county on 22 December 1852. [*See* King County.]

Pilchuck (Snohomish). Mountain, creek, and community take their names from the Chinook jargon words *pil,* meaning "red," and *chuck,* meaning "water," because of the rust-colored stream.

Pillar Rock (Wahkiakum). Community named for a nearby tall, slender rock in the Columbia River, a distinctive landmark noted by Lewis and Clark, Wilkes, and other navigators and travelers.

Pilot Point (Kitsap). Wilkes named the area to mark his meeting with the first officer of the Hudson's Bay Co. steamer *Beaver,* who, as a courtesy, piloted the American squadron down sound to Nisqually. [*See* McNeil Island.]

Pine City (Whitman). So named because of the pine trees in the area, the community was first established as a stage station on the Texas Ferry Road from Walla Walla to Colville.

Pitt Passage (Pierce). Waterway and small island west of McNeil Island was named with a single *t* by Wilkes.

Plain (Chelan). Suggested by C. F. Rupel, postmaster, because the town is situated on a flat expanse bordered by mountains.

Plaza (Spokane). Named by first postmaster, Robert Patterson, *circa* 1878 with the Spanish term for town square which he thought meant "beautiful market place."

Plymouth (Benton). Basalt rock formations jutting into the Columbia River give rise to the town name, which was the final choice of three rock titles—the Indian name Soloosa, England's Rock of Gibraltar, and the pilgrims' landing spot.

Point Defiance. *See* Defiance, Point.

Point Disney. *See* Disney, Point.

Point Doughty. *See* Doughty, Point.

Point Grenville. *See* Grenville, Point.

Point Hammond. *See* Hammond, Point.

Point Migley. *See* Migley, Point.

Point No Point (Kitsap). Named by Wilkes because at close range it appeared to be less of a promontory than it appeared from a distance. The Indian name for the large sand spit was *hahdskus,* meaning "long nose."

Point Partridge. *See* Partridge, Point.

Point Pully. *See* Pully, Point.

Point Roberts. *See* Roberts, Point.

Point White (Kitsap). The community takes its name from its location at the southwestern tip of Bainbridge Island, which was named by Wilkes for James White, ship's forecastle captain.

Pomeroy (Garfield). County seat named for Joseph M. Pomeroy, who platted the town on 28 May 1878. Pomeroy was typical of many Washington settlers. In 1850, at age 20, he migrated from Ohio to Illinois, in 1852 to Oregon, and in 1863 to Dayton, Wash., where he operated a stage station and became a rancher.

Pomona, puh-MOH-nuh (Yakima). Railroad station Wenas, named for nearby stream called Wenass by the Indians, was renamed in 1908 for the Roman goddess of fruit trees.

Portage (King). A low, narrow strip of sand connects Vashon and Maury islands and makes Maury really a peninsula of Vashon rather than a separate island. Because the site was used as a small-boat portage by early settlers, the adjacent community was given the descriptive name. [*See* Maury Island.]

Port Angeles, AN-juh-luhs (Clallam). In 1791 Eliza named the harbor Porto de Nuestra Señora de los Angeles, or "Port of Our Lady of the Angels." The following year Spanish captains Galiano and Valdés shortened the name to Porto de los Angeles, and Vancouver cut it down to its present form. The county seat city was a federal city, similar to Washington, D.C., laid out in 1862 by executive order of President Lincoln as the site of a government lighthouse and military reservation.

Port Blakely (Kitsap). The town on Bainbridge Island took its name from Blakely Harbor, which was named by Wilkes to honor Johnston Blakely, a hero of the War of 1812. [*See* Blakely Island.]

Port Discovery Bay (Jefferson). Named Port Discovery on 2 May 1792 by Vancouver for his ship. Now officially known as Port Discovery Bay, the harbor has on its shores the communities of Port Discovery, Discovery Bay, and Discovery Junction.

Porter (Grays Harbor). Town and creek were named for pioneer settler Fairchild Porter.

Port Gamble (Kitsap). The harbor on Hood Canal was named by Wilkes to honor Lt. Robert Gamble, who was wounded in the War of 1812 sea battle between the United States frigate *President* and the British *Belvidere*. The mill community is a company town owned by Pope and Talbot Lumber Co. since its inception in 1853. Port Gamble was briefly known in its formative days as Teckalet, an Indian word for "brightness of the noon-day sun."

Port Gardner. *See* Gardner, Port.

Port Ludlow (Jefferson). Town takes its title from the harbor named by Wilkes for Lt. Augustus C. Ludlow, who was killed in the War of 1812 during the sea battle between the *Chesapeake* and the British *Shannon*.

Port Madison (Kitsap). Bay, community, and Indian reservation north of Bainbridge Island all derive their names from Wilkes, who named the bay to honor James Madison, its northern point for Thomas Jefferson, and its southern point for James Monroe. This honoring of presidents led the U.S. Coast Survey in 1856 to name the next point north of the trio President Point.

Port Orchard (Kitsap). Inlet was named 24 May 1792 by Vancouver in honor of H. M. Orchard, clerk of the *Discovery,* who discovered that a supposed cove (Rich Passage) was actually an extensive inlet. The town was platted as Sidney by developer Sidney Stephens, but in 1903, at the request of residents, the state legislature renamed it and shortly afterward made it the county seat.

Port Susan. *See* Susan, Port.

Port Townsend (Jefferson). County seat city was named for the bay on which it is situated. Vancouver named the harbor for the Marquis of Townshend. Wilkes dropped the *h,* Kellett restored the *h,* the town platters omitted it for good in 1851.

Possession Sound. The waterway between southwestern Whidbey Island and the mainland was named by Vancouver, who landed near the present site of the city of Everett on 4 June 1792 and celebrated the birthday of George III by taking possession of the land of "New Georgia" for Britain. The same day he named the sound's two harbors and the southern tip of Camano Island for fellow naval officer Sir Alan Gardner and his wife Lady Susana. [*See* Allen Point; Everett; Georgia Strait; Gardner, Port; Susan, Port.]

Potlatch (Mason). Hood Canal town is named for its location at the site of a former Skokomish Indian potlatch house. The Chinook jargon word *potlatch* means "to give" and involved a lavish feast in which chiefs demonstrated their greatness by giving expensive gifts to rivals and friends.

Poulsbo, PALZ-boh (Kitsap). An Americanization of the Norwegian word *paulsbø* suggested in 1883 by early settler and post office petitioner I. B. Moe in honor of a place near his former home in Norway.

Prescott (Walla Walla). Named in 1881 in honor of C. H. Prescott, general superintendent of the Oregon Railway and Navigation Co., who had designated the community to be the location for the railway's division shops.

Preston (King). Named in 1888 in honor of William T. Preston, an official in the Seattle, Lake Shore and Eastern Railway, which laid track to the town.

Priest Point (Snohomish). Rocky point at the northern entrance to Snohomish River was called Schuh-tlahks, meaning "stony nose," by the Indians. The present name refers to a Catholic mission established on the site in 1858. [*See* Tulalip.]

Priest Rapids Dam (Grant). The rapids on the Columbia River were named by Alexander Ross of the Astoria party in 1811 to honor a Wanapum Indian medicine man or priest who greeted the explorers with religious ceremonies that included smoking the peace pipe.

Proebstel, PROHB-stuhl (Clark). Named in honor of early pioneer John Proebstel.

Prosser (Benton). The Indians called the site Tap-tap for the falls in the Yakima River. By 1882 when Col. William Prosser established a trading post, it was called Yakima Falls. A year later, the county seat town was officially named Prosser Falls, and eventually was shortened to Prosser.

Protection Island (Jefferson). Named by Vancouver, who described it as natural protection for Port Discovery both from northwest winds and—if properly fortified—from attack by an enemy.

Puffin Island (San Juan). Derives its name from tufted puffins that nest there.

Puget Island, PYOU-juht (Wahkiakum). This small island near the north bank of the Columbia River was named by Lt. W. R. Broughton of Vancouver's command on 26 October 1792 to honor the expedition's Lt. Peter Puget.

Puget Sound. Called Whulge by the Indians, the sound bears the name of Peter Puget, a second lieutenant in Vancouver's expedition. From 19 to 29 May 1792, while the sloop *Discovery* lay at anchor off Restoration Point on Bainbridge Island, Capt. Vancouver and Lt. Joseph Baker in the ship's yawl traveled the passage west of Vashon Island. During the same ten-day period the launch and cutter under Puget's command sailed south along the main channel. Vancouver's log reads as follows: "Thus by our joint efforts, we have completely explored every turning of this extensive inlet; and to commemorate Mr. Puget's exertions, the southern extremity of it I named Puget's Sound." The captain's charts show the name applied to the area south of the Tacoma Narrows, but, in time, common usage and legal decisions resulted in extension of the name (sans apostrophe) to the whole inland sea.

Pullman (Whitman). Platted in 1882 as Three Forks for its setting at the junction of three streams, the town was renamed in 1884 for railroad sleeping-car manufacturer George Pullman in hopes that he would respond to the honor with an endowment. The city is the site of Washington State University, which was established as an agricultural college in 1892 with an enrollment of 234.

Pully, Point (King). Named by Wilkes for Quartermaster Robert Pully, the name was changed in 1975 by the WSBGN to conform to the locale's more popular community title of Three Tree Point.

Purdy (Pierce). Named for a Tacoma grocer who furnished lumber for the first schoolhouse in the area. The town is the site of Purdy Treatment Center, the state's women's prison.

Puyallup, pyoo-AL-uhp (Pierce). Founded by Oregon Trail pioneer Ezra Meeker in 1877, the town was renamed to avoid confusion caused by the national proliferation of the original name of Franklin. The town took the name of the river valley in which it lies, "as we agreed there would never be but one Puyallup." The name Puyallup was that of the local Indian tribe and was composed of two words—*pough*, meaning "generous," and *allup*, meaning "people"—as they were known to be fair and honest in their trading with other Indians.

Pysht, PISHT (Clallam). River and town near its mouth carry the Chinook jargon name for the stream, *pish* or *pysht*, meaning "fish."

𝒬

Quartermaster Harbor (King). The harbor between Vashon and Maury islands was so named by Wilkes because he had titled many places in the area for petty officers of the expedition. Points in the vicinity of the harbor named for quartermasters include Piner, Neill, Dalco, Sanford, Southworth, Williams, Heyer, Pully, Robinson, and Henderson. Other petty officers whose names were point sources in the southern Puget Sound area were William Richmond, boatswain's mate, and Artemus Beals, captain of the hold.

Queets (Jefferson). Town, river, and mountain are named after the Quaitso Indians, who lived along the river's banks and were closely related to the Quinault tribe immediately to the south.

Quilcene, KWIL-seen (Jefferson). Town, river, bay, and mountain all derive their name from that of the band of Twana Indians who lived in the Dabop Bay area. The name comes from the Indian word *quil-ceed-o-bish*, meaning "salt-water people."

Quillayute River, KWIL-uh-yoot (Clallam). Named for the Indian tribe residing at the mouth of the river or vice versa. The meaning of the Indian term *quileute* is uncertain, but the original natives in the area are reputed to have called the river by that term and described it as the "river with no head" because of its scant six-mile flow from a pool formed by the confluence of the Soleduck and Bogachiel rivers through the Quillayute Indian Reservation to the Pacific Ocean. Others have contended—perhaps too conveniently— that the word meant "joining," as the Muddy Water (Bogachiel) and Sparkling Water (Soleduck) rivers merge into the Join Together (Quillayute) River.

Quimper Peninsula (Jefferson). The area between Port Discovery Bay and Port Townsend Harbor honors Spanish explorer Manuel Quimper, who visited the locality in 1790. Wilkes attempted to rename it Dickerson Peninsula after Secretary of the Navy Mahlon Dickerson, who appointed him commander of the exploration expedition in 1838. But the Spaniard's name, which had earlier been usurped from nearby New Dungeness Bay by Vancouver, was officially affixed to the peninsula by the U.S. Coast Survey.

Quinault, kwin-AWLT (Grays Harbor). Town, lake, river, and Indian reservation derive their names from Kwinaithl, the name of the largest village of the Indian tribe residing in the Quinault River Valley and the coastal area between Raft River and Joe Creek.

Quincy (Grant). While no factual explanation exists as to the name's source, the community generally believes that it was named by the daughter of railroad magnate James J. Hill. Supposedly, when the pair stepped off the train during a brief water stop and found that the spot had no name, Hill suggested that the girl christen it. She chose the present name after a city in the East, but which one is unknown. Approximately 15 states have communities named Quincy; the first was named in Maine in 1792 for Col. John Quincy, while others adopted the name as an honor to President John Quincy Adams.

R

Raft Island (Pierce). Small island in Carr Inlet named for its appearance.

Rainier, ray-NIR (Thurston). Town situated on Tenalquot Prairie was named for Mt. Rainier.

Rainier, Mt. (Pierce). The state's highest mountain is a dormant volcanic peak that towers 14,410 feet above sea level. With approximately 34 square miles of ice mantle, it is one of the world's most extensive single-peak glacier systems. It was first sighted by white man (Vancouver) on 7 May 1792. It was designated the nation's fifth national park in 1899. Its name has been—and still is—a matter of conjecture, confusion, and argument. Each Indian tribe had a slightly different title for the peak, but most were variations of Tah-ho-mah, with meanings that ranged from simply "the mountain" to "snowy mountain" and "near to sky." Vancouver named it for the grandson of Huguenot refugees whose French name was anglicized in pronunciation to "Rainy-er" and Americanized to "Ray-neer." Since British Adm. Peter Rainier gained fame for defeat of American colonists in the Revolutionary War, the name has been deemed inappropriate and subjected to agitation for change. Among the alternate names suggested are Tacoma, Tahoma, Lincoln, Harrison, and Harding. [*See* Tacoma.]

Ralston, RAWL-stuhn (Adams). Wheat-shipping station named by H. R. Williams for a brand of wheat cereals.

Randle (Lewis). Named after the Randle family, who were early settlers in the Rainey Valley area.

Ravensdale (King). Located in the heart of the Black Diamond–Franklin–Ravensdale coal field, the town title derived from word association of the Dale Coal Co. name with the flocks of ravens that fed on grain spilled from boxcars on the Northern Pacific Railroad that ran through the community. Prior to adoption of its present name, it was called Leary after the Leary Coal Co.

Raymond (Pacific). Town at the mouth of the Willapa River was named for L. V. Raymond, the first postmaster.

Reardan (Lincoln). Once called Capp's Place, the town was given its present name to honor a civil engineer of the Central Washington Railway. He arranged for a station at the townsite-to-be when settlers dug a well to prove that water was available.

Redmond (King). Settled in 1871 by William W. Perrigo and Luke McRedmond, the town was first called Salmonberg because of the large number of spawning salmon that came up the Sammamish Slough. It was renamed Melrose for Perrigo's former home town in Massachusetts, and finally Redmond after McRedmond, who platted the townsite in 1891 and served as its first postmaster.

Redondo, ri-DAHN-doh (King). Originally called Stone's Landing and subsequently Stones after S. P. Stone, who settled there in 1872. When Stones converted itself into Puget Sound's amusement center in 1904, the name was changed to capitalize on the reputation of California's amusement-park town of Redondo Beach.

Reiter, REYE-ter (Snohomish). Railroad station community named in 1906 for Charles G. Reiter of East Orange, N.J., who was president of the Bunker Hill Mining and Smelting Co.

Renton (King). Originally called Black River Bridge, the present city came into being with the discovery of coal in nearby hills by Dr. M. Bigelow in 1853. Platted in 1876, the town was named for

Capt. William Renton of the Port Blakely Mill Co., one of the founders of the Renton Coal Co.

Republic (Ferry). The Indians called the trail junction site Kleopus, meaning "valley of the cliffs"; early prospectors called their tent city Eureka after the gulch in which the first gold strike was made; but when the county seat town was platted in 1896, it was named for the Republic Gold Mine.

Restoration Point (Kitsap). An anchorage on the southeastern tip of Bainbridge Island was so named by Vancouver in honor of Restoration Day, 25 May 1660, that the English celebrated to mark the return of the Stuart dynasty to the throne of England.

Retsil, RET-suhl (Kitsap). The site of the Washington veterans' home near Port Orchard was named by spelling the surname of then Governor Ernest Lister (1913–17) backward.

Revere (Whitman). The community was made the namesake of Revolutionary War patriot Paul Revere by H. R. Williams.

Rhodesia Beach (Pacific). Named for the Rhodes family, pioneer settlers at nearby Bay City.

Rice (Stevens). Named by and for the town's first postmaster, William B. Rice.

Richland (Benton). Called Chemna by the Indians and Benton Post Office by the early settlers, the town was given its present name in 1905 to honor Nelson Rich of Prosser, who helped locate the township, and who was a partner in land holdings and an irrigation company in the area. Rich, a state legislator, introduced the bill that created Benton County out of the eastern portions of Yakima and Klickitat counties. Conversion from farm community to government town to a full-fledged city resulted from the creation of the adjacent Hanford plutonium project by the Atomic Energy Commission during World War II. The city was originally incorporated in 1908, disincorporated by the AEC in 1946, and reincorporated as a first-class city in 1958. [*See* Tri-Cities.]

Richmond Beach (King). Waterfront town was named in 1889 after Richmond, England, birthplace of an early resident.

Richmond Highlands (King). Community was named to indicate its position on the bluff above Richmond Beach.

Rich Passage (Kitsap). Southern entrance to Port Orchard was named Rich's Passage by Wilkes in honor of the expedition's botanist William Rich.

Ridgefield (Clark). The original name of Union Ridge was changed to the present title in 1890 because of the townsite's location in a flat field on a ridge.

Riffe, RIF (Lewis). Formerly Davisson Lake, the name was changed by WSBGN in 1976 to commemorate the former town of Riffe flooded over by construction of Tacoma City Light's Mossyrock Dam in 1968. Honors F. L. Riffe, pioneer settler and Baptist minister. [*See* Kosmos.]

Riparia, ri-PAIR-ee-uh (Whitman). The name was coined from the Latin word *riparius,* which refers to river bank, because of the town's position on the bank of the Snake River.

Ritzville (Adams). County seat town was named in honor of Philip Ritz, who homesteaded the site in 1878.

Riverside (Okanogan). Named for its position on the bank of the Okanogan River.

Robe (Snohomish). Named after an early settler.

Roberts, Point (Whatcom). The point and community are at the tip of a two-and-one-half-mile-square peninsula cut off from the United States mainland by the forty-ninth parallel on the north and by Boundary Bay on the east. The only entry is through Canadian and United States customs. It was named by Vancouver for the previous commander of the H.M.S. *Discovery,* Capt. Henry Roberts.

Roche Harbor, ROHSH (San Juan). The resort town on the harbor of the same name at the northwestern extremity of San Juan Island was named in 1858 in honor of Richard Roche, who served in San Juan waters under British Capt. Henry Kellett in 1846 and Capt. James C. Prevost in 1857–60. It was the site of a Hudson's

Bay Co. trading post established in 1850. From 1886 to 1940 it was the home base of the Roche Harbor Lime and Cement Co., the largest lime producer west of the Mississippi. The community which grew up around the lime works was a company town owned by John S. McMillan. The former Tacoma attorney entertained the elite, including President Theodore Roosevelt, at his lavish Afterglow Manor estate. The senior McMillan and his sons were ardent Masons and built a seven-pillared edifice, commemorating the fraternal order's concepts of family unity, that serves as a family mausoleum.

Rochester (Thurston). Originally named Moscow by a Russian immigrant, the town was renamed with the establishment of the post office in 1890 for the New York home town of another settler.

Rockford (Spokane). So named by pioneer D. C. Farnsworth in 1879 because of many fording spots used to cross Rock Creek, which ran through the center of town.

Rock Island (Douglas). The city was so named because of its proximity to the Rock Island Rapids in the Columbia River.

Rocklyn (Lincoln). Named Rockland by the railroad in 1898, the community was given the present more euphonious title when the post office was established a year later.

Rockport (Skagit). Founded in the 1890s, the community derived its name from the many large rocks at the boat landing site on a point in what is now Skagit Steelhead Park.

Rodna, RAHD-nuh (Spokane). Railway station community was named by the Spokane, Portland and Seattle Railroad after one of its officials.

Rolling Bay (Kitsap). Named Murden's Cove in 1856 by the U.S. Coast Survey, but known locally as Rowles's Bay after a white settler and his Indian wife who resided on its shore. The community was given its present descriptive name with establishment of the post office in 1892.

Ronald (Kittitas). Named for Alexander Ronald, a Scots immigrant, who served as superintendent of the Northwestern Improvement Co. coal mines in the Roslyn-Ronald area.

Roosevelt (Klickitat). Named in honor of President Theodore Roosevelt.

Rosalia (Whitman). Named in 1872 to honor Rosalia Favorite, wife of the first postmaster.

Rosario Strait, roh-ZAIR-ee-oh (San Juan). Literally "Rosary Strait," the water boundary between San Juan and Skagit counties is one of the relocated Spanish names. Eliza had originally named the waterway Boca de Fidalgo and had called the present Gulf of Georgia, Gran Canal de Nuestra Señora del Rosario la Marinera. In 1841, Wilkes named it Ringgold Channel in honor of his expedition's Lt. Cadwalder Ringgold. In 1847, British Capt. Henry Kellett clarified the charts in his pro-British–anti-American fashion by confirming Vancouver's Gulf of Georgia at its present location and replacing both Eliza's Bay of Fidalgo and Wilkes's Ringgold Channel with the shortened version of the former gulf title.

Rosburg, RAHS-berg (Wahkiakum). Adaptation of the name of Christian Rosberg, the community's first postmaster.

Rosedale (Pierce). Named by early settlers for the profusion of wild roses growing along the shores of Henderson Bay.

Rose Hill (King). Name was derived from the formal, old-country style rose gardens on the estate of Peter Kirk, the English industrialist who founded nearby Kirkland in 1886.

Roslyn (Kittitas). Named in 1886 by the general manager of the Northern Pacific Railroad's coal mine for his sweetheart in Roslyn, N.Y.

Roy (Pierce). First called Muck, the settlement was renamed for the son of James McNaught, who platted the townsite *circa* 1884.

Royal City (Grant). Once the area around a post office known by the topographically descriptive title of Red Rock, the new town situated on Royal Flat adopted its present name in 1957 when it became the center of a prime agricultural area as a result of government reclamation projects in the Royal Slope district.

Ruby (Pend Oreille). Town was named in 1905 for nearby Ruby Creek, which had been named by prospectors who found red garnets while panning the stream. An Okanogan County town of Ruby, named after a nearby mine, vanished after a drop in silver in the early 1890s, a flood in 1894, and a fire in 1900.

Ruff (Grant). Named for Gotfred Ruff, on whose property the town was located.

Ruston (Pierce). Named in honor of W. R. Rust, one of the founders of the smelter there and president of the Tacoma Smelting Co.

Ruth Prairie (Thurston). Originally named Ruth's Prairie in 1850 for early settler B. F. Ruth. Subsequently, apostrophe and letter "s" dropped in accordance with national geographic board policy of eliminating possessives in the interest of simplification and clarity.

Ryderwood (Cowlitz). Established in 1923 as Ryder Wood, the logging town was named for William Ryder, woods superintendent for Longbell Lumber Co. [*See* Longview.]

Rye (Kittitas). Named after Rye, N.Y., by H. R. Williams.

Sacajawea, SAK-uh-juh-WEE-uh (Franklin). State park southeast of Pasco and reservoir behind Ice Harbor Dam are named for the Shoshone Indian "Bird Woman," who (with her husband Toussaint Charbonneau, a French-Canadian *voyageur*) accompanied the Lewis and Clark Expedition.

Saddlebag Island (Skagit). So named because of its shape. [*See* Dot Island.]

Safari Island. *See* Spieden Island.

Saginaw, SAG-in-aw (Grays Harbor). Named for the Saginaw Timber Co. that logged the area and which, in turn, was given its name by principals formerly associated with the Michigan town of the same title. Its Ojibwa Indian word meaning is "place of the Sac Indian tribe."

St. Andrews (Douglas). Named *circa* 1890 for Capt. James St. Andrews, a Civil War veteran who was the community's first postmaster.

St. Helens, Mt. (Skamania). The Indians called it Lawala Clough, or "smoking mountain," and its present name was bestowed by Vancouver to honor the British ambassador to the court of Madrid.

St. John (Whitman). Named in 1888 by the Oregon Railway and Navigation Co. for early settler E. T. St. John.

Salkum, SAL-kuhm (Lewis). Town name is an Indian word meaning "boiling up" and refers to a series of waterfalls in a nearby stream that was first called Salkum Creek and then renamed Mill Creek when a grist mill was established near its confluence with the Cowlitz River.

Salmon La Sac, SA-muhn-lah-SAK (Kittitas). The French word *sac* translates as "bag" or "sack" and, hence, explains the name affixed to the lake by trappers, who saw Indians net salmon in sack-like baskets woven of cedar bark.

Salsbury Point (Kitsap). The tip of land north of the Kitsap Peninsula approach to the Hood Canal Floating Bridge was named by Wilkes to honor Francis Salsbury, a captain of the top in the expedition crew.

Samish Bay, SAM-ish (Skagit). The bay, an island, a river, a summer community, and a railroad station all bear the name of the Indian tribe, said to number over 2,000 people in the 1840s, that originally occupied the coastal areas of Skagit and Whatcom counties. The name is derived from the Skagit Indian word *samens,* meaning "hunter."

Samish Lake (Whatcom). The lake and the community on its northern shore bear the name of an Indian tribe that also served as the name source for several points in adjacent Skagit County.

Sammamish, Lake, suh-MAM-ish (King). A large lake east of Lake

Washington that is the setting for a suburb of Seattle and environs. The name is that of an Indian tribe that lived on the lakeshore in earlier times.

Sammamish Slough (King). A slow-flowing river that drains Lake Sammamish and joins it to the northern end of Lake Washington. The name is that of an Indian tribe that occupied the area of the lake and river, and is derived from two words—*samena,* meaning "hunter," and *mish,* meaning "people."

San de Fuca, SAN-duh-FYOO-kuh (Island). Community on Penn Cove on the east side of Whidbey Island was platted and named in 1889. The name apparently combines—purposely or mistakenly—the titles of the Strait of Juan de Fuca and the San Juan Islands.

San Juan County, san-WAHN; 172 sq. mi.; 39th in size; seat: Friday Harbor, San Juan Island. Smallest of the state's counties, it is comprised of 172 named islands (and reputedly 300 more rocky "islands" at low tide). Following the Forty-ninth Parallel Boundary Treaty of 1846, both the British and the American governments claimed possession of the islands. The English offered land-grant inducements to prospective British settlers; the Americans attempted to collect taxes; the British appointed a justice of the peace to enforce the Queen's Law; and on 15 June 1858 American homesteader Lyman Cutler precipitated war: he shot a Hudson's Bay Co. pig that rooted in his potato patch. The British ordered Cutler's arrest, and the American hid out in the forest. The Americans sent one ship and 461 soldiers under Capt. George Pickett (who later, as a major-general, led the famous Confederate charge at Gettysburg). The British retaliated with a naval force of five ships and 2,000 men. The "Pig War" became a checkmate situation, and for 12 years the two countries jointly occupied the islands while a boundary commission debated the issue. Finally it was referred to international arbitration, and on 21 October 1872 German Emperor William I ruled in favor of the United States. On 31 October 1873 the territorial legislature organized the archipelago into San Juan County, bounded on the west and north by Haro Strait and separated on the east from mainland county islands by Rosario Strait.

San Juan Island (San Juan). Discovered and named in 1791 by the Spanish, this second largest island in the archipelago is the site of the county's largest town and county seat, Friday Harbor. San Juan Island was the "battleground" of the Pig War of 1812.

San Juan Islands (San Juan). Island group in north Puget Sound discovered in 1791 by Lopez Gonzales de Haro, who was under the command of Spanish explorer Francisco Eliza. The latter, in turn, sailed under authority of the viceroy of Mexico, one Señor Don Juan Vicente de Güemes Pacheco de Padilla Horcasitas y Aguayo. With an eye to future patronage, Eliza charted the island group as Isla y Archiepelago de San Juan. For the next two years from headquarters at Nootka Sound on Vancouver Island, Eliza and his colleagues—Salvadore Fidalgo, Jacinto Caamaño, Cayetano Valdés, and Dionisio Alcalá Galiano—liberally bestowed portions of the viceroy's name, one another's names, and a variety of Spanish words on a host of geographic features in the northern Puget Sound and Vancouver Island waters. The British next named some new discoveries and renamed some that the Spanish had titled. Hudson's Bay Co. affixed the name Bellevue to San Juan Island; George Vancouver in 1792 applied Georgia Strait to the previously named waterway north of the San Juans. However, it was cosmographer Charles Wilkes of the U.S. Navy and commander of the American Survey Expedition who fouled up the nautical charts in 1841. A worshiper of the navy and its heroes of the War of 1812, Wilkes, perhaps unaware of the Spanish effort as he had been at sea since 1838, named everything he saw in the Pacific Northwest that was not recorded on British charts and maps. He (re)named the San Juans as the Navy Archipelago and recorded that the individual islands "have been named for distinguished officers late of the U.S. Naval Service, viz, Rodgers, Chauncey, Hull, Shaw, Decatur, Jones, Blakely, Perry, Sinclair, Lawrence, Gordon, Percival and others." In 1847 Capt. Henry Kellett was directed by the British Admiralty to rework the charts to eliminate confusion and duplication. He protected most English names, dropped many of the American names, and reinstated or relocated the original Spanish titles. Thus, Canadian waters show an English-Spanish influence, the San Juan area has a Spanish-American-English flavor, and the southern Puget Sound region is primarily American—and all three name belts are heavily salted with Indian words. [*See* Orcas Island.]

Sanpoil River, SAN-POIL. Tributary of the Columbia River in Okanogan and Ferry counties bears the name of an Indian that inhabited the region.

Sappho, SA-foh (Clallam). Name is that of an ancient Greek poetess who lived on the Isle of Lesbos in 600 B.C. and was known for her erotic love lyrics.

Sares Head, SAIR-es (Skagit). A bluff on the southern shore of Fidalgo Isalnd was named by Wilkes to honor Henry Sares, captain of the expedition's *Top.*

Satellite Island (San Juan). Named for the H.M.S. *Satellite* commanded by James Charles Prevost, British commissioner in the San Juan boundary dispute. Adjacent Prevost Harbor and Charles Point also honor the admiral.

Satsop, SAT-suhp (Grays Harbor). The town was named for the river which bears the name of a band of Indians living along the tributary of the Chehalis River. The name is derived from *sachap* or *sats-a-pish,* meaning "on a stream."

Satus Pass, SAY-tus (Yakima). Name source for the pass, a tributary of the Yakima River, and a rural community is a band of Yakima Indians known as the Setaslema or "people of the rye grass prairie."

Sauk, SAWK (Skagit). River, mountain, and rural community bear the name of the Sah-kee-ma-hu band of the Skagit Indian tribe, which lived in the area.

Scandia (Kitsap). Originally known as Frykholm after John Frykholm, a retired Lutheran preacher, who built the first dock and store, the community was renamed to reflect its Swedish heritage.

Scarboro Head (Pacific). Bluff near the town of Chinook was named for James Scarborough, a former Hudson's Bay Co. ship captain who homesteaded the area and served as a Columbia River pilot.

Scatchet Head, SKAT-chit (Island). This southernmost bluff of Whidbey Island reflects one of the early spellings of the name of the Indian tribe inhabiting the area. [*See* Skagit County.]

Schwarder (Yakima). Named for a leading resident, John C. Schwarder.

Seabeck (Kitsap). Named for Seabeck, Me., home of Marshall Blinn, who established a sawmill at the site in 1857. It was the site of a world-renowned port, a major Puget Sound shipyard, two mills producing 80,000 board feet of lumber per day, and a logging camp with 600–1,000 permanent population in the 1880s. On 6 August 1886 fire destroyed most of the town, the Washington Mill Co. relocated its operation at Port Hadlock, and the place became a ghost town. In 1914 the 700-acre townsite was purchased by the Coleman family of Seattle and established as an interdenominational church conference grounds.

Seabold (Kitsap). Name of tidal shore was coined by William Bull in 1894 as a play on the phrase "the sea is bold."

Seattle, see-AT-uhl (King). Largest city in the state, the seat of King County was settled 13 November 1851 at Alki Point on the southern shore of Elliott Bay. On 15 February 1852 three of the pioneers—A. A. Denny, W. N. Bell, and C. D. Boren—staked claims on the eastern shore of the bay along what is now the city center waterfront. On 23 May 1852 the town was platted and named for the chief of the Duwamish and Suquamish tribes. His name has been variously spelled and pronounced: See-alt, See-ualt, See-yat, Sealth, and Se-at-tlh. Christened Noah Sealth by Catholic Father Modeste Demers, the chief remained a friend of the white settlers until his death in 1866. Indian names for portions of what is now Seattle include Mulckmukum, Duwamps, and Tzee-tzee-lal-itch. [*See* Alki Point; Suquamish.]

Seaview (Pacific). In 1871, J. L. Stout erected a summer hotel on

400 wilderness acres facing the ocean, and in time the town that grew up around the resort adopted its name.

Sedro Woolley, SEE-droh WOO-lee (Skagit). Settled in 1878 by David Batey and Joseph Hart, who sold 40 acres to Mortimer Cook in 1884. The latter laid out a townsite and named it Bug. In wrathful indignation the other settlers threatened to add the prefix "hum" to the town sign. The townswomen suggested—but misspelled— the Spanish word *cedro,* meaning "cedar," as a more appropriate name that tied in to nearby Cedar Mountain. As the head of navigation on the Skagit River, the town prospered, particularly during the Mt. Baker gold rush days. In 1889 the Great Northern and Northern Pacific railroads established a junction north of Sedro, and P. A. Woolley platted a townsite there bearing his surname. To mitigate the high costs of duplicate governments, the adjacent towns were incorporated (with a now forgotten hyphen) as Sedro-Woolley in 1890.

Sekiu, SEE-kyoo (Clallam). Name derived from an Indian word meaning "calm water."

Selah, SEE-luh (Yakima). Name is an Indian word meaning "smooth water" and was applied by the natives to the stretch of the otherwise turbulent Yakima River that runs quietly past the present townsite.

Selleck, SEL-ek (King). Named for Superintendent F. L. Selleck of the Pacific States Lumber Co., the town's main industry.

Semiahmoo Bay, sem-ee-A-moo (Whatcom). Bay derives its name from that of the Semiamu Indians, who lived on its shores. It purportedly translates as "half-moon," but its pronunciation and meaning is so similar to the English "semi-moon" that the definition is suspect—particularly since early ethnologists failed to make note of any phonetic coincidence. Semiahmoo community on the peninsula that separates the bay and Drayton Harbor was a boom town during British Columbia's Fraser River gold rush in 1858. [*See* Drayton Passage.]

Sequim, SKWIM (Clallam). Name derived from the Indian word *such-e-kwai-ing,* meaning "quiet water."

Shaw Island (San Juan). Wilkes named the island for Capt. John D. Shaw, who served under Decatur in the second war with Algiers (Barbary pirate states), May–June 1815.

Shelton (Mason). County seat town was named for David Shelton, who homesteaded the area in 1853. A former fur trapper, Indian fighter, and gold prospector, Shelton was a member of the first territorial legislature and succeeded in having his home area organized as Sawamish County. At a later session he sponsored a bill to change the county name to Mason in honor of Charles H. Mason, the territory's first secretary. The town is the site of the Washington State Correctional Center for rehabilitation of criminals. [*See* Mason County; Oakland Bay.]

Shilshole Bay, shil-SHOHL (King). An adaptation of Shul-shale, the name of an Indian tribe that lived in the area. The bay is west of the Hiram M. Chittenden Locks that link Lake Washington and Puget Sound. The area was the site of the city of Ballard, now a part of Seattle. Platted as Gilman Park in 1888 by Capt. W. R. Ballard, the town was renamed Ballard the following year by the Seattle, Lake Shore and Eastern Railway, which built a spur station there.

Shine (Jefferson). Postal officials rejected the proposed name of Sunshine for the Hood Canal community, but accepted this abbreviated form.

Shuksan, Mt., SHUCK-san (Whatcom). Skagit Indian name meaning "rocky and precipitous."

Si, Mt., SEYE (King). Backdrop for the town of North Bend, the frequently climbed mountain was named in 1862 for Josiah "Si" Merrit, early settler in the area.

Sifton (Clark). Named in 1908 for Dr. Sifton of Portland, a stockholder in the Oregon-Washington Corp. that operated an electric line to Vancouver.

Silvana, sil-VAN-nuh (Snohomish). First known as Stillaguamish.

With the coming of the railroad in 1892, the town was retitled to fit its wooded setting and as a tie in to early settler Michael Sill. The name is one of a variety of place names in the nation coined from the Latin root word *sylvan* or *silvan,* meaning "forested."

Silver Creek (Lewis). Named in 1868 by John Tucker for the small stream that flowed by the edge of town.

Silverdale (Kitsap). The original intent in 1889 was to call the town Goldendale, but when it was found that the name duplicated that of a city in eastern Washington, it was decided simply to drop down a notch on the precious-metal scale by substituting silver for gold.

Silverlake (Cowlitz). Lake-shore community adopted the color-descriptive name of Silver Lake.

Simcoe, Fort (Yakima). Now a state historical park, the post housed the U.S. 9th Infantry Regiment during 1856–59, and subsequently served as an Indian agency and school. Located on the Yakima Indian Reservation, the fort derived its name from the tribal name for the valley: Sim-kwee, combining "waist" and "spine," a descriptive term for the saddle in a long ridge rimming the valley to the north.

Similk Beach, SEYE-milk (Skagit). An Indian word meaning "salmon."

Sinclair Inlet (Kitsap). Named by Wilkes to honor the expedition's George T. Sinclair, acting master of one of the ship's crews.

Sinclair Island (Skagit). Named by Wilkes for Arthur Sinclair, Sr., captain of the 32-gun *General Pike* at the outbreak of the War of 1812.

Skagit County, SKA-jit; 1,735 sq. mi.; 22nd in size; seat: Mount Vernon. Created 30 November 1883 by the territorial legislature out of the southern portion of Whatcom County. The county was given the name of the Indian tribe that had inhabited the area. The meaning of the name is lost, but under various early spellings it was affixed to several geographic points in the region: Scaadget

Bay, Scaget River, Skait Island, and Scatchet Head (still in use) at the southern tip of Whidbey Island.

Skagit Island (Skagit). Located due east of Deception Pass, the island was charted by Wilkes as Skait Island, another spelling variation of the name of the Indian tribe inhabiting the area. The island is at mid-point on the western shore of the Swinomish Indian Reservation where many Skagits now reside.

Skagit River (Skagit). The 125-mile-long river rises in British Columbia and flows through Whatcom and Skagit counties into Skagit Bay, which lies between Whidbey Island and the mainland. Named after Indians that lived along its banks.

Skamania, skuh-MAY-neeuh (Skamania). Town was originally called Butler until residents petitioned for a change that would serve as a geographic tie in to the county.

Skamania County; 1,676 sq. mi.; 34th in size; seat: Stevenson. Organized by the territorial legislature on 9 March 1854 and given the Indian name meaning "swift waters," referring to the Columbia River that forms its southern border.

Skamokawa, skuh-MAH-kuh-way (Wahkiakum). An Indian word meaning "smoke over the water," referring to morning fog at the confluence of Skamokawa Creek and the Columbia River. The term was adopted as his name by the chief of a small band of Chinooks residing there and, in turn, was taken by the white settlers as the title of their town. Because the creek was the early community's main thoroughfare, it was nicknamed "Little Venice."

Skipjack Island (San Juan). Wilkes originally named the two adjacent islands north of Waldron Island as the Ship Jack Islands, probably after fish found in the area and commonly referred to as shipjacks. In 1853 the U.S. Coast Survey noted the contrast in the islands' appearances and renamed them Wooded and Bare islands. The latter was renamed as Penguin Island in 1858. Subsequently, the islands were officially charted under the present names of Skipjack and Bare islands.

Skokomish River, skoh-KOH-mish (Mason). Name of the area's resident Indian tribe is based on two of their dialect words—*s'ḵaw,* meaning "fresh water," and *mish,* meaning "people." The river rises in the Olympic Mountains and enters Hood Canal near Union.

Skookumchuck River, SKOO-kuhm-chuhk. The Chinook jargon words *skookum,* meaning "strong," and *chuck,* meaning "water," combine to title this stream in Lewis and Thurston counties as "swift river."

Skykomish (King). Town is named for the river that rises in the Cascade Mountains and joins the Snoqualmie River to form the Snohomish River. The name is from the Indian words *skaikh* and *mish,* meaning "inland people."

Smith Cove (King). Cove at the northeastern corner of Elliott Bay was named in honor of Dr. Henry A. Smith, who settled there in 1853.

Smith Island (Island). Smith and Minor islands, joined at low tide, were named by the Hudson's Bay Co. and have been important navigation points since the early 1800s. Eliza called the pair Islas de Bonilla for Antonio de Bonilla, while Wilkes named the larger one Blunt's Island to honor the expedition's Midshipman Simon F. Blunt.

Smyrna, SMER-nuh (Grant). Named for the Turkish city by H. R. Williams.

Snake River. Greatest tributary of the Columbia River was named Lewis River on 21 August 1805 by Capt. William Clark to honor his fellow explorer, Capt. Meriwether Lewis. However, usage of the term "Snake" for the Indians and the region where it flows resulted in adoption of the present name for the 1,038-mile-long river that rises in Yellowstone National Park.

Snee Oosh Beach, SNEE-ohsh (Skagit). A former portion of the Swinomish Indian Reservation purchased by whites in 1925 still carries its native name, meaning "beach facing west."

Snohomish, snoh-HOH-mish (Snohomish). The city was founded *circa* 1860 by E. C. Ferguson and E. F. Cady as a trading post on the Snohomish River to serve both local settlers and the river commerce plying the Snoqualmie and Snohomish valleys. Initially known as Cadyville, it was subsequently called Snohomish City prior to adoption of the present shortened name.

Snohomish County; 2,100 sq. mi.; 13th in size; seat: Everett. Name of the Indian tribe that inhabited the Snohomish River Valley and the area now occupied by the city of Everett. Early spellings of the word, which lacks clear-cut definition (the final syllable, *mish,* means "people"), include: Sinnahamis, Sinahomis, and Ashnuhumsh.

Snoqualmie, snoh-KWAHL-mee (King). River, falls, pass, and two towns—Snoqualmie and Snoqualmie Falls—among other geographic points, carry the name of the Indian tribe of the area. The original native term was *sdoh-ḳwahlb-bhuh,* based on the word *sdoh-ḳwahlb,* meaning "moon," the legendary life source of the tribe.

Soap Lake (Grant). Resort town on the shores of the southernmost lake in the Grand Coulee. The name is derived from the bitter taste and soapy feel of the water that wind whips into a sudsy foam. The lake is of volcanic origin as evidenced by black basalt cliffs along its shore and the heavy concentration of minerals and salts in the water. To the Indian and the pioneers, as well as today's health-seekers, the spot was famous as a health spa.

Sol Duc Hot Springs, SAWL-duhk (Clallam). Indian for "sparkling water." [*See* Soleduck River.]

Soleduck River, SAWL-duhk (Clallam). Initially called Sol Duc, as currently are the hot springs. *Sol duc* is an Indian term meaning "sparkling water," as the natives believed that the water had magical medicinal powers. [*See* Quillayute River.]

South Bend (Pacific). The county seat town situated on a southerly bend in the Willapa River began as a sawmill settlement in 1860.

South Prairie (Pierce). Established as Melrose in 1884 and renamed in 1889 as a geographically descriptive tie in to its location on South Prairie Creek.

Southworth (Kitsap). Located on Point Southworth, which was named by Wilkes for Quartermaster Edward Southworth.

Spanaway (Pierce). A lake and a southern suburb of Tacoma bear as their name a corruption of the Indian word *spanuch* of undetermined meaning. Hudson's Bay Co. records show "two plows sent to Spanuch" 26 April 1849. More recent folklore contends that it is the reverse spelling of the Indian name for the lake: *yawanaps,* meaning "beautiful water."

Spangle (Spokane). Named for William Spangle, a Civil War veteran, who homesteaded in 1872 and platted the townsite in 1886. Located on the Colfax-Spokane stage route, it was rated in 1881 as the second best [major] town in the county.

Spee-Bi-Dah (Snohomish). A small community on the Tulalip Indian Reservation and a needle-like rock projecting from a bluff on the Port Susan shore are both named with a phonetically spelled Indian term meaning "small child." [*See* Tulalip.]

Spieden Island, SPEE-duhn (San Juan). Named by Wilkes for William Spieden, purser of the *Peacock,* the privately owned island is still officially Spieden despite attempts in 1970 to change the title to Safari Island to promote awareness of the 2,000-acre island as a "shoot-for-pay" hunting reserve.

Spirit Lake (Skamania). The community name is derived from that of the lake, which the Cowlitz Indians called *nyas cultus,* meaning "very bad" lake. Apparently early volcanic action of Mt. St. Helens caused steam spouts and erratic currents on the lake's surface, which frightened the natives. Early settlers adapted the concept of the Indian name to the appropriate English word when a post office was established in 1903.

Spokane, spoh-KAN (Spokane). Fur traders first applied the name Spokane to the Indians of the area, to the river along which they lived, and then to the trading post, Spokane House (1810–26), built below Spokane Falls at the junction of the Spokane and Little Spokane rivers. The derivation of the name stems from the tribe's leader, who identified himself to early trappers as Illim-Spokane or "chief of the sun people." Settlement of the present city site began in the early 1870s, and the town was born 13 February 1878, when James Nettle Glover filed the plat of Spokane Falls. In 1881 the town was incorporated, and in 1891 the name was shortened to Spokane.

Spokane Bridge (Spokane). So named because it was the site of the first bridge across the Spokane River. A trading post was built in 1862, the bridge was completed in 1864, and a post office was established in 1867.

Spokane County; 1,763 sq. mi.; 19th in size; seat: Spokane. The county, named for an Indian tribe, was carved out of Walla Walla County in 1858 and included all of the area east of the Columbia River and west of the Rocky Mountains between the Canadian border and the Snake River. When Oregon became a state in 1859 and was assigned its present boundaries, Spokane County was enlarged to encompass all of Idaho and part of Wyoming. Formation of Idaho Territory in 1863 reduced Spokane County in size accordingly. The following year Spokane County was abolished altogether via incorporation into Stevens County. However, the same year (1864) it was re-established. It next had as much trouble with its seat as it had experienced with its boundaries. In 1864 Spokane was named the county seat. In 1880 Cheney won the seat by vote. Spokane charged election fraud and claimed victory in the recount. Cheney challenged the matter in court. The judge procrastinated, so Cheney citizens abducted both the county records and the auditor. In 1881 the court ruled in favor of the kidnapers. Cheney's victory was short-lived, as Spokane, "The Capital City of the Inland Empire," became the official and final county seat by ballot in 1886. [*See* Cheney.]

Sprague (Lincoln). Named to honor Gen. John W. Sprague, director of the Northern Pacific Railroad.

Springdale (Stevens). Originally called Squire City after early homesteader Charles O. Squire, the town name was changed when the adjacent Sheep Creek was renamed Spring Creek.

Squamish Harbor, SKWAH-mish (Jefferson). Harbor south of the Olympic Peninsula approach to the Hood Canal Floating Bridge is an alternate spelling of the Salish Indian word *suquamish* designated to the site by Wilkes. [*See* Suquamish.]

Squaw Canyon (Whitman). Several lesser features in the state, including a railroad junction and three creeks, carry the general term applied to Indian women. The word was initially adopted from the Algonquin-speaking tribes of the East Coast: the Delaware's *ochqueu* and the Massachusetts' *eshqua,* meaning "female animal."

Squaxin Island, SKWAWX-uhn (Mason). Island, reservation thereon, and the present tribal name are derived from the Indians' original name for themselves: Skwaks-namish, which literally meant "alone people."

Stampede Pass (King). The pass was discovered in 1881 by Virgil C. Bogue as part of the route survey for construction of the Northern Pacific Railroad over the Cascade Range. A foreman's effort to speed up construction work with a "no work, no eat" edict precipitated a stampede of laborers back to the valley and resulted in the naming of the pass, and eventually a railroad tunnel and the small community near its west entrance.

Stanwood (Snohomish). Settled in 1866 as a trading post on marshy land at the mouth of the Stillaguamish River, the resultant community was built on reclaimed land and called Centerville. In 1877 merchant D. O. Pearson became postmaster and renamed the town to honor his wife Clara's maiden name.

Star (Okanogan). Named for R. W. Starr, orchardist who owned the land through which the Great Northern Railroad was built.

Starbuck (Columbia). Named to honor a New Yorker, General

Starbuck, an official and stockholder of the Oregon Railway and Navigation Co., who gave the town its first church bell.

Startup (Snohomish). Platted as the townsite of Wallace in 1890 because of its location at the confluence of the Wallace River with the Skykomish River. To avoid misdirection of mail to Wallace, Ida., the logging town was renamed in 1901 for George G. Startup, manager of the Wallace Lumber Co.

Stayman (Chelan). Railroad station named for a variety of apple grown in the area.

Steamboat Rock (Grant). Situated in the Grand Coulee seven miles south of Coulee City, the mesa was once an island in the prehistoric Columbia River. It was so named because of its fancied resemblance to a steamboat.

Stehekin, steh-HEE-kin (Chelan). Town and river bear the Indian word meaning "the way," as the river bed forms a pass to Lake Chelan.

Steilacoom, STIL-uh-kuhm (Pierce). Town founded in 1851 and the adjacent lake derive their name from the Indian word *tchil-ac-cum,* meaning "pink flower," which was the name of an Indian village originally located at the townsite. The village was variously recorded as Chelakoom, Chilacoom, and Chielcoom, and its chief's name was reported to be Tail-a-koom. Nearby Western State Hospital is situated on the site of Fort Steilacoom, occupied by the U.S. Army from 1849 to 1868 and donated to the state in 1874 for a mental hospital.

Steilacoom, Fort (Pierce). Established in July 1849 by U.S. Army troops to protect settlers from raids by hostile Indians, principally those under Chief Patkamin. Acquired by the state after the army abandoned the post in 1869, it continues the original name of Fort Steilacoom to differentiate it from the nearby town of Steilacoom.

Stella (Cowlitz). Named for original storekeeper-postmaster's daughter Stella Packard.

Steptoe (Whitman). Town, creek, rapids in the Snake River, and a butte [formerly Pyramid Peak] honor Lt. Col. Edward J. Steptoe, who campaigned against marauding Indians in the Walla Walla Valley in 1857. On 17 May, Steptoe and 150 soldiers equipped with two howitzers were defeated by 1,000 Palouse Indians in the Battle of Te-Hots-Nim-Me, marked by Steptoe Memorial Park at Rosalia.

Stevens, Lake (Snohomish). Lake east of Everett was originally named Stevens Lake in 1859 to honor Isaac I. Stevens, first governor of Washington Territory. Subsequently, the two-word name of the lake and the town on its shore was reversed.

Stevens County; 2,486 sq. mi.; 5th in size; seat: Colville. Organized by the territorial legislature on 20 January 1863. It was named in honor of Isaac Ingalls Stevens, the first territorial governor and supervisor of Indian affairs, who served from 1853 until 1857, when he was elected to represent the territory in Congress. General Stevens was killed leading an assault against the Confederates in the Civil War battle of Chantilly, 1 September 1862.

Stevens Glacier (Pierce). One of the glaciers comprising 34 square miles of ice mantle on Mt. Rainier honors Hazard Stevens, son of former governor Isaac Stevens, who with P. B. Van Trump made the first ascent to the summit in 1870.

Stevenson (Skamania). County seat town was platted in 1894 by George H. Stevenson, who migrated to Washington Territory from Missouri in 1880.

Stevens Pass. Named for construction engineer John F. Stevens, who supervised the Great Northern Railroad track-laying over and through the Cascades.

Stillaguamish River, stil-uh-GWAH-mish (Snohomish). Meaning "river people," the Indian word is the name of the tribe who lived in the area of the river's three forks.

Stillwater (King). Rural community south of Duvall that was platted as a town in 1910 by H. Butikafer. He named it to honor owners and workers of a nearby logging camp, who hailed from

Stillwater, Minn., which, oddly enough, had been named for a timber company.

Strait of Juan de Fuca. *See* Juan de Fuca, Strait of.

Strandell, STRAN-duhl (Whatcom). Named in honor of Andrew Strandell, who built a sawmill there in the 1890s.

Stratford (Grant). Named, *circa* 1890, by the Great Northern Railroad purportedly after Stratford-on-Avon, resulting in the building of the Shakespeare Hotel and ceremonial exchanges of correspondence with the English town.

Strawberry Island (Skagit). Vancouver named Strawberry Bay and Cypress Island in 1792, but left this adjacent island nameless. Wilkes found wild strawberries on the island and named it Hautboy (pronounced HO-boy) after the variety of strawberry. However, the more common name has been officially affixed to the island.

Strawberry Island (Skamania). Mile-long island in the Columbia River was so named 2 November 1805 by Lewis and Clark because it was "covered with grass and a great number of strawberry vines."

Stretch Island (Mason). Small island in Case Inlet was named by Wilkes for gunner's mate Samuel Stretch. In 1878 Walter Eckert established a vineyard on the island. Viticulture expanded, and the place became known locally as the Isle of Grapes, home of the Island Belle variety.

Stuart Island (San Juan). Named by Wilkes for Frederick D. Stuart, captain's clerk of the expedition.

Sucia Island, SOO-shuh (San Juan). Called Isla Sucia by Eliza. In Spanish *sucia* means "dirty," or in the nautical sense "foul," and is a description of the reefs and hidden rocks surrounding the island.

Sultan (Snohomish). The river derived its name from Indian chief Tseul-tud. Placer gold mining in the 1880s fostered the town, which was named for the river.

Sumas, SOO-muhs (Whatcom). International boundary town,

mountain, prairie, and stream all derive their name from a Cowichan Indian band that lived in the area. The native meaning of the word is "big level opening."

Summit (Pierce). So named because it was located at the high point of the tracks of the Tacoma-Puyallup electric rail line of the 1890s.

Sumner (Pierce). Platted by John F. Kincaid on the donation land claim of his father William Kincaid and named to honor Bostonian and slavery opponent Charles S. Sumner, who served in the United States Senate from 1851 to 1874.

Sunnyside (Yakima). Town was laid out and named by Walter N. Granger, president of the Sunnyside Canal Co. in 1893. [*See* Granger.]

Suquamish, soo-KWAH-mish (Kitsap). First called Bartow after the agent in charge of adjacent Port Madison Indian Reservation, the town was renamed in 1910 when Seattle mayor-to-be Ole Hansen developed it as a summer residence area. The town area is the site of the 900-foot-long cedar-plank communal dwelling in which Chief Seattle was born *circa* 1786 to Suquamish Chief Schweabe and Wood-sho-lit-sa of the Duwamish tribe, and where Seattle later maintained the headquarters for his band and subchiefs. On the hill above the town is Seattle's grave, with a marker tombstone that reads: "Seattle, Chief of the Suquampsh and Allied Tribes. Died June 7, 1866. The firm friend of the whites and for him the City of Seattle was named by its founders. Sealth. Baptismal name Noah Sealth." [*See* Blake Island; Seattle.]

Susan, Port. The waterway between Camano Island and the mainland which forms the boundary between Island and Snohomish counties was named by Vancouver for Lady Susana Gardner. [*See* Gardner, Port; Possession Sound.]

Sutherland, Lake (Clallam). Named for John J. Sutherland, who was the first to build a cabin on its shores in 1886.

Sutico, SOO-ti-koh (Pacific). Name coined from the first two letters in Sunset Timber Co., which logged in the area.

Swinomish Slough, swin-OH-mish (Skagit). The channel linking

Skagit and Padilla bays is a veritable salt-water river whose flow alters direction with each change of tide. On its east bank is the main town of La Conner. On its west bank is the Swinomish Indian Reservation named for a branch of the Skagit Indian tribe.

Sylvan (Pierce). Community on Fox Island was called Sylvan Glenn in 1888 because of its forest setting, but shortened with establishment of the post office in 1891.

𝕥

Tacoma, tuh-KOH-muh (Pierce). Called Chebaulip by the Indians, the locality of the county seat city was first settled in 1852 by Nicholas DeLin. Indian hostilities forced the settlers to abandon the area, and it was not until 1864 that the first permanent homesteader, Job Carr, took up land in what is now Tacoma. In 1868 Gen. Morton M. McCarver, a professional town developer, arrived from Portland in search of a site that might serve as the terminus of the proposed Northern Pacific Railroad. He found it on the south shore of Commencement Bay. He bought Carr's property and platted a townsite under the proposed name of Commencement City. At the suggestion of others, the name was changed to Tacoma, the Indian name for Mt. Rainier mentioned in Theodore Winthrop's famous book on the Pacific Northwest *The Canoe and the Saddle*—and, thus, the City of Destiny was born. Lumber mills sprang up, the harbor became a regular port of call for sailing vessels, and, in fulfillment of McCarver's foresight, the railroad arrived in 1893. [*See* Mt. Rainier.]

Taholah, tuh-HOH-luh (Grays Harbor). Situated at the mouth of the Quinault River on the Quinault Indian Reservation, the town was named for Quinault tribal chief Taholah.

Tahuya, tuh-HOO-yah (Mason). Name of a creek and community derived from the Twana Indian words *ta* and *ho-i,* meaning "that done," in reference to some notable occurrence that took place at the site long ago.

Tampico, tahm-PEE-koh (Yakima). Community was named by pioneer settler A. D. Elgin for an Oregon town in which he had previously lived.

Tanglewilde (Thurston). The name of this unincorporated Olympia suburb was coined and trademarked by home builder Alvin H. Thompson as a tie-in to the rustic setting of the development.

Tatoosh Island, ta-TOOSH (Clallam). While *ta-toosh* is a Chinook jargon word meaning "breast," derived from the eastern Chippeway, a similar word *to-tooch,* meaning "thunder bird," exists in the Wakashan language spoken by the Nootka Indians on Vancouver Island, of which the Makah are the southern branch. Though from the air the cape area is vaguely breast-shaped in outline, it is more logical that the Makah took the name from their own language rather than from the trade jargon. The assumption is enhanced by the fact that other names in the immediate area—all sites of Makah villages—are from their own language: Ho-selth, Ba-a-dah, Arch-a-wat, Waadah. [*See* Alava, Cape; Neah Bay; Ozette, Lake.]

Tekoa, TEE-koh-uh (Whitman). Although early references listed the name as an Indian word, it is actually a biblical name suggested by Mrs. Dan Truax, wife of the first postmaster. It is a Hebrew word meaning "settlement of tents" and appears several times in the Old Testament, for example, in Samuel XIV :2-20.

Tenino, ti-NEYE-noh (Thurston). Erroneously claimed to originate from the railroad jargon ten-nine-oh variously reported to be the number of a survey station at the site, Northern Pacific engine Number 1090 that regularly stopped at the station, and even the number of a boxcar on the siding there in the early days. Admittedly the town came into existence in the early 1870s as a railroad construction camp during the laying of track from Kalama to Tacoma, but the location already bore its present name. In the Chinook jargon *tenino* means "fork" or "junction," and the name was given to a point on an old Indian trail which was so called and subsequently so marked on territorial maps when the trail was expanded to a military road during the Indian Wars of 1855–56.

Termination Point (Jefferson). The tip of land north of the Olympic Peninsula approach to the Hood Canal Floating Bridge was named by Wilkes, as it marked the northern end of Hood Canal. Actually Termination Point (by Squamish Harbor) and Foulweather Bluff (known in the past as Suquamish Head) mark the western and eastern banks of the only entrance to Hood Canal.

The Brothers. *See* Brothers, The.

The Dalles Dam, DALZ (Klickitat). So named because of its location across a rocky narrows in the Columbia River called La Grande Dalle de Columbia by French fur trappers. In French the word *dalle* means "flag stone," and the term "The Dalles" was applied to describe the flat-rock rapids. [*See* Dallesport.]

The Narrows. *See* Narrows, The.

Thomas (King). Named for former Kentuckian John M. Thomas, who settled in the White River Valley in 1853 and served as county commissioner in 1857–59.

Thompson Cove (Pierce). Named for the Reverend Robert Thompson, chaplain of the British vessel *Fisgard* that sailed Puget Sound in 1846.

Thornton (Whitman). Once prosperous railroad wheat-shipping center was named for its position on Thorn Creek.

Thorp (Kittitas). Named for early settler Milford A. Thorp.

Thrall, THRAWL (Kittitas). Named in 1889 to honor an official of the Northern Pacific Railroad.

Three Lakes (Snohomish). Community was named by John Lauderyon in 1903, because of its proximity to Panther, Flowing, and Storm lakes, for a town similarly situated in his home state of Wisconsin.

Three Tree Point. *See* Pully, Point.

Thurston County; 717 sq. mi.; 32nd in size; seat: Olympia. Created on 12 January 1852 by the Oregon Territorial Legislature. Initially, the proposed act specified that the new county, broken off from Lewis County, be named Simmons County for Michael T. Simmons, leader of the first party of Americans to settle in the Puget Sound basin. [*See* Tumwater.] However, prior to passage, the act was amended to change the name to honor Samuel R. Thurston, Oregon's first delegate to Congress.

Tieton, TEYE-uh-tuhn (Yakima). Town takes its name from that of the river, which, in turn, was christened in the 1880s with an adaptation of an Indian word meaning "roaring water."

Tiffany Mountain (Okanogan). Named for Will Tiffany who, with his two brothers, maintained a camp at the mountain's base. A close relative of the New York jewelry family, he was killed while serving with Teddy Roosevelt's Rough Riders in Cuba during the Spanish-American War.

Tiflis, TIF-luhs (Grant). H. R. Williams chose the name because many of the farmers in the area had migrated from that sector in Russia. The Georgian capital city's name literally means "warm springs."

Tiger (Pend Oreille). Named for one of the townsite's early settlers, George Tiger, who operated a steamboat stop called Tiger Landing.

Tillicum, TIL-i-kuhm (Pierce). Adaptation of the Chinook jargon word *tilakum,* meaning "friend."

Tilton River (Lewis). The tributary of the Cowlitz River was named in 1857 for James Tilton, surveyor-general of Washington Territory.

Toandos Peninsula, toh-AHN-dohs (Jefferson). Peninsula separating Dabop Bay from Hood Canal proper was named by Wilkes. It is apparently a phonetic adaptation of *tu-an-hu,* meaning "portage," the name source of the Twana Indian tribe which inhabited the area.

Toe Point (San Juan). The eastern end of Patos Island was assigned its descriptive name by British charts of 1888.

Tokeland, TOHK-luhnd (Pacific). The town on the northern shore of Willapa Bay and nearby Toke Point were named for Chief Toke, who was reputedly the town drunk, the region's fastest canoe paddler, and a garrulous source of Indian legends.

Toledo (Lewis). Named after the river boat *Toledo* that served the community in 1879.

Tolmie Peak, TOHL-mee (Pierce). Named for Hudson's Bay Co. surgeon William Fraser Tolmie, who in 1833 was the first white man to attempt to climb Mt. Rainier.

Tolt River, TOHLT (King). This tributary of the Snoqualmie River was initially shown on territorial maps of 1857 as the Tolthue River. The Snoqualmie Indians called the place H'lalt, which in their guttural tongue is pronounced similarly to the river's present name. A town called Tolt at the junction of the Tolt and Snoqualmie rivers was renamed Carnation in 1917 to honor the nearby dairy farm of a major milk producer. [*See* Carnation.]

Tonasket, tuhn-AS-kuht (Okanogan). Town and stream 15 miles to the north were both named for Chief Tonascutt of the Colville Indian tribe.

Toppenish, TAH-puhn-ish (Yakima). The town which borders the Yakima Indian Reservation derives its name from the native word *qapuishlema,* meaning "people from the foot of the hills."

Totten Inlet (Thurston). One of the southern arms of Puget Sound named by Wilkes to honor an officer of the expedition. [*See* Budd Inlet.]

Touchet, TOO-shee (Walla Walla). Tributary of the Walla Walla River and a town at its mouth bear an adaptation of the Indian word *tousa,* meaning "curing salmon before a fire."

Toutle, TOO-tuhl (Cowlitz). The tributary of the Cowlitz River and the small community on its banks derived their name from a spoken-usage adaptation of the Indian word *hullooetell,* referred to by Lewis and Clark as the name of an Indian tribe living on the upper reaches of the Coweliskee (Cowlitz River).

Towal, TOW-uhl (Klickitat). Former town and present railroad station named for an Indian chief.

Tracy Point (Stevens). The point jutting into Loon Lake was cleared by Washington's most infamous badman, Harry S. Tracy, before he launched on his outlaw career.

Tracyton (Kitsap). The Dyes Inlet community was named in honor of Benjamin Franklin Tracy, secretary of the navy under President Benjamin Harrison, 1889–93.

Trentwood (Spokane). It was originally called East Trent because of its proximity to the then larger town of Trent. While the latter underwent a series of name changes to end up as Irvin, East Trent centered a series of satellite communities: a railroad station known as Steno in honor of a court stenographer who doubled as an orchardist along the spur, and a community known as Trentwood Orchards because of the presence of both lumber and fruit trees. In 1917 the stenographer and many of the fruit trees died, so the railroad and the various communities amalgamated under the present name.

Tri-Cities (Benton and Franklin). Richland, Kennewick, and Pasco comprise the entity commonly called the Tri-Cities. The first two, located in Benton County, were initially small agricultural communities, while Pasco was the Franklin county seat and site of railroad yards. In 1943 the Atomic Energy Commission constructed a plutonium-producing facility, the Hanford Works, north of Richland. The three towns boomed and grew into one crescent-shaped population center extending along both banks of the Columbia River. [*See* Hanford.]

Trinidad (Grant). Named for a Colorado town because of similar topographic features.

Trout Lake (Klickitat). Town derives its name from a nearby lake and a stream that flows into the White Salmon River.

Tucannon, too-KAN-uhn (Columbia). Name is derived from the Nez Perce word *tu-ḳan-non,* meaning "bread root creek." The difficult Indian pronunciation resulted in many different spellings for both the name of the Snake River tributary and the railroad station: Tchannon, Tookanan, and even Two Cannon.

Tuckey, TUHK-ee (Jefferson). Initially called Tuckey's Landing, the resort community bears the name of John F. Tuckey, former Maine resident, who took up a donation claim on the eastern side of Port Discovery Bay in 1852.

Tukwila, tuhk-WIL-luh (King). Formerly known as Garden City, its name was adapted in 1905 from the Indian word *tuckwilla,* meaning "land of hazelnuts."

Tulalip, too-LAY-lip (Snohomish). Small inlet north of the Snohomish River estuary, which the Indians named *duh-hlay-lup,* meaning "small mouth bay." The name was extended to the adjacent 18,191-acre Indian reservation surrounding the bay and to a small town on the northern shore of the bay. Development of the area began with the establishment of a Catholic mission at Priest Point and an Indian cemetery at Mission Beach by Father E. C. Chirouse in 1858, and designation of Tulalip as one of the state's four Indian Agency headquarters in 1859.

Tumtum (Stevens). Small community on a noisy stretch of the Spokane River derives its name from the Chinook jargon word meaning "heart," called *thum[p]-thum[p]* by the Indians.

Tumwater (Thurston). The oldest American settlement in the Puget Sound country is on the falls of the Deschutes River. The Indians called it *spa-kwatl,* meaning "falls"; the French *voyageurs* named it *deschutes,* or "falls"; their Hudson's Bay Co. superiors, contemplating the erection of a sawmill there, wrote of it as Puget Sound Falls; Wilkes referred to it as Shute's River Falls; and in the Chinook jargon the name was Tum-wat-er. Michael Troutmans Simmons, leader of the Americans who settled there in 1845, called the site New Market. Later the name was changed to Tumwater, as it likened the sound of falling water to the repeated throb of a human heart, which was expressed in the jargon as *thum-thum.*

Turn Island (San Juan). Initially, it was thought by Wilkes to be a part of San Juan Island and was named Point Salsbury in honor of Francis Salsbury, captain of the expedition's vessel *Top.* In 1858 the British found it actually to be an island (with adjacent dangerous rocks that are submerged except at low tide) and renamed it Turn Island and Turn Rocks to mark the proper channel.

Twisp (Okanogan). Named Gloversville in 1898 for the first postmaster. To avoid confusion with Clover in the same county, the town adopted the name of the nearby Twisp River, which derived its name from the Indian word *twitsp*.

Tyee, TEYE-ee (Clallam). Logging community and lake bear the Chinook jargon word for "anyone of superior status"; literally "chief."

Tyler (Spokane). Town was originally called Stephens. On arrival of track, the Northern Pacific Railroad named its station Tyler, purportedly as a tongue-in-cheek honor for a Montana resident who collected damages from the line. To avoid the confusion of two names for the same spot, the residents renamed the community.

U

Uncas, UHN-kuhs (Jefferson). The Cooper family, early settlers on whose land the original town was platted, selected the community name from the Leatherstocking Tales by James Fenimore Cooper. Uncas was a Mohegan chief who fought on the side of the English during King Philip's War in 1675. His name meant "the fox who circles," and monuments to him exist in Norwich, Conn., and Cooperstown, N.Y.

Underwood (Skamania). Named for Amos Underwood, who settled on the Columbia River at the townsite in 1875.

Union (Mason). Originally a logging center on Hood Canal, the town was named Union City in 1858. The latter word was dropped by the post office in 1904, and the town fathers followed suit some years later.

Union, Lake (King). Small lake north of Seattle's central business district that the Indians called Kah-chung, or "small lake." It received its present name in 1854 from Thomas Mercer, who predicted that it would one day join the waters of Lake Washington with those of Puget Sound—which it now does via the Lake Washington Ship Canal to the east and Salmon Bay Canal and the Hiram M. Chittenden Locks to the west. [See Washington, Lake.]

Union Gap (Yakima). Formerly known as Yakima City, the town's present name stems from its location near the gap in the Ahtanum Ridge that connects the central and lower portions of the Yakima Valley. [See Yakima.]

Uniontown (Whitman). Controversy over a suitable town name in 1879 was settled by Father Joseph Cataldo, S.J., who suggested the present title, as the community was a junction point of creeks and roads and because a Union Creek and a Union Flat already existed in the area.

University Place (Pierce). Laid out and named as the projected, but never realized, home of the University of Puget Sound.

Urban, ER-buhn (Skagit). The town on Sinclair Island was named by L. V. Stenger in honor of his son Urban Stenger.

Useless Bay (Island). Two shallow bays on the southern shore of Whidbey Island bear the same name but in different languages. Wilkes so named Useless Bay for its lack of shelter from storms, while the adjacent bay was given the Chinook name of *cultus,* meaning "bad" or "worthless," for the same reason by Capt. George Davidson of the U.S. Coast Survey. [See Cultus Bay.]

Usk, UHSK (Pend Oreille). Named in 1890 by George H. Jones for the Usk River in Wales.

Utsalady, uht-suh-LAD-ee (Island). Former sawmill community on Camano Island was named for the Indian word meaning "land of berries."

Vader, VAY-der (Lewis). The town's original name, Little Falls, duplicated that of another community served by the Northern Pacific Railway. The Northern Pacific suggested Sopenah; the townsfolk countered with Toronto. Finally the matter was referred to the state legislature in 1913, and as a compromise the town was named to honor an elderly German who was one of the early settlers. Mr. Vader was not flattered, but outraged, and promptly moved to Florida.

Vail (Thurston). Former community surrounding logging operation shops was named for the family that donated the townsite land to the Weyerhaeuser Co.

Valhallas (Jefferson). Multiple peaks in the Olympic Mountains and similarly titled geographic entities throughout the state derive their names from the great hall of the Norse god Odin: Valhalla, the mythical heaven of the Vikings.

Valley (Stevens). So named because of its setting in the Colville Valley.

Valleyford (Spokane). Words comprising the name explain its origin.

Van Buren (Whatcom). Rural community was named for an early settler who established the post office that once served the locality.

Vancouver, van-KOO-ver (Clark). The oldest continuously inhabited white settlement in the state was established in 1825 when Dr. John McLoughlin, chief factor, moved the Hudson's Bay Co. Columbia Department Headquarters upriver from Fort George— now Astoria, Ore.—and named it to honor British explorer George

Vancouver. After the Boundary Treaty of 1846, the company gradually withdrew from United States territory south of the forty-ninth parallel and established its main trading post for the district at Victoria on Vancouver Island in British Columbia. In 1849, United States forces set up a permanent military establishment adjacent to the original fort (which Hudson's Bay abandoned entirely in 1860), calling it Columbia Barracks and, subsequently, Vancouver Barracks. Over the years under British and American rule, the post—now a national historic site—played host to many famous men: David Douglas for whom the Douglas fir tree is named; frontiersman Jedediah Smith; missionaries Marcus Whitman and Henry Spaulding and their wives; Catholic Fathers Blanchet and Demers. Famous American military men assigned to the post at some time during their careers include: Ulysses S. Grant, George Armstrong Custer, Philip Sheridan, and George C. Marshall. In the early days, resentment of past British domination—and, more recently, hopes of avoiding geographic confusion with the Vancouvers in Canada—have prompted sporadic and unsuccessful attempts to change the town's name to Vancouver City, Columbia City, and Columbia.

Van Horn (Skagit). Named for its first settler and platter of the townsite, James V. Van Horn.

Vantage (Kittitas). Community derived its name from that of Mr. Van Slack, who operated a ferry from the site until the high steel bridge across the Columbia River was built in the early 1930s.

Van Wyck, van-WIK (Whatcom). Named in 1889 for early settler Alexander Van Wyck.

Van Zandt, van-ZANT (Whatcom). Named in 1892 for J. M. Van Zandt, the community's first postmaster.

Vashon, VASH-ahn (King). The island was originally named Vashon's Island by Vancouver on 29 May 1792 to honor his close friend Capt. James Vashon of the British Navy, who rose from lieutenant to commander for his heroics against rebel vessels during the American Revolutionary War. Two communities, Vashon and Vashon Heights, are named for the island on which they are located.

Vassar (Adams). Now reduced to the status of a railroad stop, the town was named for Vassar, the women's college in Poughkeepsie, N.Y., by H. R. Williams.

Vaughn (Pierce). Town and bay named for W. D. Vaughn, who settled a claim on Case Inlet in 1851. Following service in the Indian Wars of 1855–56, he moved from Vaughn Bay to Steilacoom, where he worked as a gunsmith.

Veazey, VEE-zee (King). Rural community was named in 1880 for Thomas Veazie of the Veazie and Russell Logging Co.

Vega, VAY-guh (Pierce). Community on Anderson Island derived its name from Vegatorp, Sweden, home town of its first postmaster.

Velox, VEL-ox (Spokane). Railroad station in the Spokane Valley named by clerk Arthur S. Glendinning for his father's prize race horse, a trotter named Harry Velox, *circa* 1912.

Vendovi Island, ven-DOH-vee (Skagit). The namesake of a Fijian cannibal taken captive by Wilkes during a stopover en route to the Pacific Northwest. The prisoner, held in low esteem by Wilkes's men, in turn viewed the local natives with utter contempt. By the time the expedition returned to the East Coast on 10 June 1842, Vendovi's health had failed, and he died in the naval hospital in New York. [*See* Henry Island; Viti Rocks.]

Venersborg (Clark). Community was established in 1909 by the Swedish Land and Colonization Co. on land owned by a farmer named Vener. The company principals combined the similar name of their home town of Vanersborg, Sweden, with the surname of the previous owner, to coin the new town's name.

Venice, VEN-uhs (Kitsap). Known as Venice Landing, site of the longest wharf (780 feet) on Puget Sound, *circa* 1908, the Bainbridge Island community is the namesake of California's once artificially canaled copy of the Italian city.

Veradale (Spokane). Namesake of Miss Vera McDonald, whose father helped plat the district in 1911, the town was first called Vera but changed to Veradale in 1923.

Vesta (Grays Harbor). Rural community was named for a creek which, in turn, was named for Vesta Dwinelle by her husband when he explored the area in 1882.

Victor (Mason). Source of the name selected in 1892, when ships delivered mail to the "pigeon hole" post office housed in the community's general store, was unrecorded and is unknown by proprietor-postmaster's son E. H. Sisson of Olympia.

Viti Rocks, VEE-tee (Whatcom). Named by Wilkes for Viti Levu, one of the Fiji Islands that was the home of a cannibal the expedition took prisoner and brought to the Pacific Northwest. [*See* Henry Island; Vendovi Island.]

WW

Wagnersburg (Chelan). Railway station community named for E. Wagner, orchardist in the Wenatchee and Okanogan valleys.

Wahkiacus, wah-KEYE-uh-kuhs (Klickitat). Named for an aged Indian woman, Sallie Wahkiacus, who held a tribal allotment of government land in the area when the railway station town was founded.

Wahkiakum County, wuh-KEYE-uh-kuhm; 269 sq. mi.; 38th in size; seat: Cathlamet. Created by the territorial legislature as Wakiacum [*sic*] County, 25 April 1854. The name is derived from that of a Kathlamet Indian village on the north bank of the Columbia River near Puget Island. The Wakaiyakam villagers comprised a sub-tribe of the Kathlamet Indians and were identified by the name of their first leader, Chief Wakaiyakam. [*See* Cathlamet.]

Waitsburg (Walla Walla). Town was originally called Delta, but the name was changed by ballot in 1868 to honor Sylvester M. Wait, who had constructed a flour mill at the site in 1864.

Waldron Island (San Juan). Named by Wilkes for two members of the expedition's force: Thomas W. Waldron and R. R. Waldron, captain's clerk of the *Porpoise* and purser of the *Vincennes,* respectively.

Walla Walla, WAW-luh-WAW-luh (Walla Walla). Mentioned by Lewis and Clark in 1806 as Wollah Wollah and Wollaw Wollahs, the name was first applied to the valley and river, and subsequently to county, fort, and city. The name comes from the Nez Perce word *walatsa,* meaning "running water," with repetition loosely translating as "many waters." In 1855, Isaac I. Stevens, who doubled as territorial governor and superintendent of Indian affairs, made a peace treaty with the "Walla-Walla, Cayuses, and Umatilla Tribes and Bands of Indians" at the present townsite. Despite this, the Indian War broke out, and Lt. Col. Edward J. Steptoe built a fort at the treaty campsite around which the city developed. It was known first as Walla-Walla, then Steptoeville, Wieletpu, and, finally, Walla Walla—the name under which it was incorporated on 11 January 1862. The county seat city is the location of the state penitentiary, which in criminal jargon is appropriately nicknamed "The Walls." [*See* Wallula.]

Walla Walla County; 1,288 sq. mi.; 27th in size; seat: Walla Walla. Created by the territorial legislature on 25 April 1854, to consist of all land between the Cascade and Rocky Mountains and the Columbia River and the Canadian border. The name is a derivative of the Nez Perce and Cayuse Indian word, *walatsa,* meaning "running water." The Nez Perce called the Indians of the area Walawalapu, or "Little River People." In several native dialects *walla* means "water," and duplication of the term signifies diminution as "little rapid river" or gives it the plural connotation "many waters." In the 1850s there was agitation to create a new and separate territory out of the eastern portions of Washington and Oregon, specifically out of the mammoth Walla Walla County, an area now generally known as the Inland Empire. Among the names suggested for the new entity (to be based on geographic similarity), the most frequently mentioned was, and is, the state of Lincoln.

Wallula, wuh-LOO-luh (Walla Walla). From 1818 to 1855 fur trappers operated a fortified trading post at the mouth of the Walla Walla River. It was historically known as "old" Fort Walla Walla, although the North West Fur Company builders called it Fort Nez Perce. Following the cessation of Indian hostilities, the city of Walla Walla grew up around Lt. Col. Steptoe's new fort, while the town of Wallula developed at the site of the old fort. The town's name means the same in Walla Walla language as the city's does in the Nez Perce tongue: "many waters." [*See* Walla Walla.]

Wanapum Dam (Grant). Dam, reservoir, and state park bear the name of an Indian tribe known as the "river people" that inhabited the Columbia River valley from Pasco to Vantage.

Wapato, WAH-puh-toh (Yakima). Located in an area heavily populated with Indians and devoted to growing potatoes, the town was named in 1902 with a variation of the Chinook jargon word *wappatoo*, meaning "potato."

Warden (Grant). Another of the 32 railway stations in the state named by H. R. Williams. This time the name honored an easterner who had invested extensively in the line's stock.

Washington. On 8 February 1853 a bill calling for creation of Columbia Territory out of the lands of the Oregon Territory lying north of the Columbia River was introduced in the United States Congress. Representative Richard H. Stanton of Kentucky amended the bill to replace *Columbia* with *Washington,* "as we already have a territory [District] of Columbia . . . but we have never yet dignified a territory with the name of [George] Washington." Within five minutes the bill was approved by the House, and on 2 March it was passed by the Senate and signed by President Millard Fillmore. The new territory extended from the Pacific Ocean to the Rocky Mountains between the forty-ninth parallel of north latitude and the forty-sixth parallel of south latitude and the

Columbia River. The present eastern boundary was established in 1863 via creation of Idaho Territory on 3 March 1863. The Enabling Act for admission of Washington to statehood was approved by President Grover Cleveland on 22 February 1889, and, after framing and approval of its constitution, Washington was proclaimed the forty-second state by President Benjamin Harrison on 11 November 1889. [*See* Monticello.]

Washington, Lake (King). To the Indians it was It-how-chug, meaning "large lake." It was called Lake Geneva after its counterpart in Switzerland by euphemistic Isaac N. Ebey, but mapmakers followed the lead of Seattleites, who called it Lake Duwamish to honor local Indians. At a pioneer picnic in 1854 Thomas Mercer suggested that it be called Lake Washington after George Washington, for whom the new Washington Territory had been named the previous year. He also suggested that the smaller lake to the west be named Union, as it would one day unite the larger lake's waters with those of Puget Sound.

Washougal, WAW-shoo-guhl (Clark). River and town derive their name from the Indian word meaning "rushing water." Lewis and Clark named the river Seal River as they saw a large number of seals at its mouth. The town initially was called Parker's Landing.

Washtucna, wawsh-TUHK-nuh (Adams). Bears the name of a lake 12 miles distant in Franklin County that was named after a Palouse Indian chief.

Wasp Island (San Juan). Wilkes collectively named a group of small islands in the San Juan Channel as the Wasp Islands to honor the sloop *Wasp,* captained by Master Commandant Jacob Jones in the War of 1812. Subsequently, the group was individually named as Bird Rock and Brown, Cliff, Nob, Reef, Yellow, and Wasp islands. [*See* Jones Island.]

Waterman (Kitsap). Named in 1904 in honor of Delos Waterman, an early homesteader in the area.

Waterville (Douglas). The county seat has had three names. In

1884, as main stopping point en route to the Okanogan country, it was called Okanogan City. It was next called Jumper's Flat as a commentary on the claim-jumping prevalent prior to the arrival of the railroad. It was finally platted under its present name when a 30-foot well produced water.

Wauconda, waw-KAHN-duh (Okanogan). Named by an early resident after Waconda, Ore. The original Willamette Valley community has long passed into oblivion, but the Indian term meaning "up valley" lives on in its adopted home.

Waukon, WAU-kahn (Lincoln). Established as a station when the Spokane, Portland and Seattle Railroad was built, and purportedly named after an Indian chief.

Wauna, WAW-nuh (Pierce). In 1906 Mary R. White, first postmistress, adopted as the town name an Indian word meaning "strong and mighty."

Waverly (Spokane). Named in 1879 for two residents' former home town in Iowa.

Wawawai, wuh-WAH-ee (Whitman). Name adapted from an Indian word meaning "council ground."

Welcome (Whatcom). Rural community and former post office location was named by and for its first postmaster John Welcome Riddle.

Wellpinit, WEL-pin-it (Stevens). Initially the site of a Presbyterian mission on the Spokane Indian Reservation, the community's name source is undetermined. An unsubstantiated local belief suggests that the name is an adaptation of an Indian term referring to "two small creeks in a valley."

Wenatchee, wuh-NACH-ee (Chelan). The name of the county seat city, river, mountain, and national forest, among other geographic points, is an adaptation of the Yakima Indian word *wenatchi,* meaning "river flowing from canyon."

Westlake (Grant). So named because of its location on the western shore of Moses Lake.

West Point (King). Point of land at the northern entrance to Seattle's Elliott Bay was so named by Wilkes because it runs virtually due west from Magnolia Bluff. The Indian name for the sand spit was *pḳa-dzeltco,* meaning "thrust far out."

Westport (Grays Harbor). The self-proclaimed salmon sport-fishing capital of the world is situated on a cove on the western side of Chehalis Point Spit, which separates Grays Harbor from the southwest. The area, originally known as Peterson's Point after Glenn Peterson who settled there in 1858, was the site of Old Fort Chehalis and the county's first schoolhouse. Nearby is Twin Harbor State Park.

Whatcom, Lake, WHAHT-kuhm (Whatcom). The lake, named for a Nooksack Indian chief, flows via Whatcom Creek into Bellingham Bay near the site of the 1852 town of Whatcom and present-day Bellingham.

Whatcom County; 2,151 sq. mi.; 11th in size; seat: Bellingham. Created by the territorial legislature on 9 March 1854 and given the name of a Nooksack Indian chief, whose name was said to mean "noisy water." Whatcom was also the name of the first town on Bellingham Bay which, through consolidation with Sehome and Fairhaven, became the present-day city of Bellingham.

Whidbey Island (Island). Named by Vancouver to honor the expedition's sailing master Joseph Whidbey, who discovered Deception Pass, the waterway that established the land mass as an island rather than a peninsula. Site of the Whidbey Island Naval Air Station, the island is the second longest in the United States mainland. [*See* Deception Pass.]

Whitcomb (Benton). Established in 1909 as Luzon, the former town was renamed in 1910 for local landowner A. Henry Whitcomb.

Whitehorn Point (Whatcom). The southern point of Birch Bay was named by Wilkes to honor Daniel Whitehorn, one of the expedition's gunners.

Whiteman's Cove (Pierce). The small cove on the eastern shore of

Case Inlet honors the first white man in the area, a homesteader named Reed, who settled there with his Indian wife.

Whites (Grays Harbor). Rural community was named by officials of the Northern Pacific Railroad in honor of Allen White, who operated a sawmill there in 1890.

White Salmon (Klickitat). River, then town, derived their name from the tremendous number of salmon—which turn white in color during spawning runs—that abounded in the river and tributaries each fall.

White Swan (Yakima). Established 13 January 1960, the Yakima Indian Reservation town was named for the Indian on whose land it stands and who served as tribal chief for 60 years.

Whitlow (Whitman). The rural community named for M. W. Whitlow, an early farmer in the area.

Whitman County; 2,167 sq. mi.; 10th in size; seat: Colfax. Organized under a territorial legislative act of 29 November 1871 and named in honor of the missionary Marcus Whitman, who with his wife and ten others was massacred by Cayuse Indians in 1847. Dr. Whitman and H. H. Spaulding and their wives, the first American women in the old Oregon Territory, had established a mission near Fort Walla Walla in 1836.

Whitney (Skagit). The town of Padilla, established in 1882 by Rienzie E. Whitney, moved closer to the newly arrived railroad in 1890 and changed its name to honor its founder.

Whittier (Kittitas). Railway station at the eastern end of Stampede Pass was named for poet John Greenleaf Whittier by H. R. Williams.

Wickersham (Whatcom). Brothers Noah and William Wickersham, who settled on the south fork of the Nooksack River *circa* 1885, donated land for the railroad right-of-way, and, subsequently, the station and post office were named in their honor.

Wilbur (Lincoln). Named for its founder Samuel Wilbur Condit in 1887. The trading post was previously known as Goosetown after Condit, who was nicknamed "Wild Goose Bill," as he had mistakenly shot another settler's tame gander while hunting Canadian honkers.

Wiley (Yakima). Named Wiley City on 6 July 1910 by Wallace Wiley to honor his pioneer father Hugh Wiley, on whose homestead the town was platted.

Wilkeson (Pierce). The former coal-mining center was named for Samuel Wilkeson, secretary of the board of the Northern Pacific Railroad that laid track to the town in 1876 and began coal-mining operations in 1879.

Willapa, WIL-uh-puh (Pacific). Town, bay, and river now all carry an adaptation of Ah-whil-lapah, the name of the Chinook Indian tribe that resided along the banks of the river that flows into the oyster-laden bay. Despite a deep-water channel into the bay, it long carried the name of Shoalwater Bay assigned by its discoverer Capt. John Meares, a retired British Navy lieutenant turned fur trader. It was described as one vast bed of oysters exposed twice daily by low tide.

Willard (Skamania). Named for early-day rancher and county commissioner Emil Willard.

Williamson Rocks (Skagit). Located off the western shore of Fidalgo Island, the jutting rocks were named by Wilkes for John G. Williamson, one of the expedition's gunners.

Wilson Creek (Grant). Community is the namesake of a creek that bears the name of an early settler.

Winesap (Chelan). Former town and railroad apple-shipping center was so titled when the name was selected by post office officials from a list submitted by Elizabeth Cole, first postmistress.

Winlock (Lewis). Named in honor of Gen. Winlock E. Miller, who was a close friend of Territorial Governor Isaac I. Stevens, an officer in the Indian War of 1855–56, and owner of the land upon which the town was built.

Winona, weye-NOH-nuh (Whitman). A Santee Indian word meaning "first-born daughter" affixed to the site by a railroad survey engineer from Winona, Minn. [*See* Lacrosse.]

Winslow (Kitsap). Named for Winslow Hall, one of the founders of Hall Brothers Marine Railway and Shipbuilding Co., the area's major industry.

Winthrop (Okanogan). Named by early settler United States Senator John Wilson, who, in his late years, could not remember the exact name source. He believed that he had named the town to honor New England author Theodore Winthrop, who journeyed over the Cascade Mountains in 1853 and subsequently lauded the Washington region in his book *The Canoe and the Saddle*.

Winton (Chelan). Platted in 1914 as Winton Place by the Winton Lumber Co.

Wishkah, WISH-kah (Grays Harbor). River and rural community carry an adaptation of the Chehalis Indian word *hwish-ḳahl,* meaning "stinking water."

Wishram (Klickitat). The town was given the name that Wilkes ascribed to an Indian village above The Dalles on the Columbia River. Purportedly the name was that of a long-dead chief. However, the Bureau of American Ethnology reports that the tribal name, in two different Indian dialects, refers to a "specie of flea or louse."

Withrow (Douglas). Named for pioneer wheat rancher J. J. Withrow.

Wollochet Bay, WOH-loh-chet (Pierce). Bay and community names derived from the Indian word *wal-atch-et,* meaning "squirting clams."

Woodinville (King). Named by early residents to honor pioneer settler Ira Woodin.

Woodland (Cowlitz). Named for its wooded setting by Christopher Columbus Bozagth, first merchant and postmaster, at the suggestion of his wife. Identically or similarly named unincorporated communities (without post offices) with the same name source exist in Pierce, Snohomish, Island, and Grays Harbor counties.

Woodmans (Jefferson). Former town on the southeastern shore of

Port Discovery Bay was named not for loggers of the area but for pioneer settler James O. Woodmans.

Woodway (Snohomish). Seattle suburban community situated south of Edmonds was named for its natural setting—tree-lined roads and small-estate-sized lots.

Worden, Fort (Jefferson). Named in honor of Adm. John L. Worden, who commanded the U.S. Navy's *Monitor* when it engaged the Confederate *Merrimac* at Hampton Roads, Va., 8–9 March 1862. [*See* Casey, Fort.]

Wright, Fort (Spokane). Named for Col. George Wright of the U.S. Army 9th Infantry, who took command of the Columbia River Military District during the Indian Wars in 1856.

Wynoochee River, weye-NOO-chee (Grays Harbor). The tributary of the Chehalis River running southeast from the Olympic Mountains is fed by the heaviest rainfall in the continental United States—average 141 inches per year. The name is an Indian word meaning "shifting" that refers to the river's course.

𝖄

Yacolt, YA-kawlt (Clark). Town took the Indian name "haunted place" for the prairie on which it is situated. A small band of Indians mysteriously lost their children while picking huckleberries, and after a futile search concluded that they had been stolen by Yacolt, the evil spirit.

Yakima, YAK-i-maw (Yakima). Yakima City was incorporated 1 December 1883, and a year later had 400 residents. In 1884 the Northern Pacific Railroad platted North Yakima four miles north and offered to give Yakima City residents an equal amount of property and to move their buildings without charge if they would transfer to the new town. A majority of the citizens agreed, and in

90 days, during the winter and spring of 1884–85, over 100 buildings —including a bank, hotels, stores, and other business structures— were moved by wagon, skids, and rollers to the new community. On 12 January 1886 the city was chartered and simultaneously named the county seat. An act of the state legislature effective 1 January 1918 dropped the word "North" from the city's name and changed the name of the older town (Yakima City) to Union Gap.

Yakima County; 4,273 sq. mi.; 2nd in size; seat: Yakima. Established by the territorial legislature on 21 January 1865 and named for the Indian tribe of the area. Early spellings of the name include Skaemena and Eyekema, with the most widely accepted meaning being "runaway," referring to the rushing waters of the Yakima River around which tribal life centered. However, many etymologists contend that the name is a corruption of *yah-ḳuh-muh,* meaning "big belly" or "pregnant one," which ties into early tribal legend.

Yarrow Point, YAIR-roh (King). Township on the eastern shore of Lake Washington was named by early-day land developer R. D. McAusland for a line in the poem "Yarrow Revisited" by English poet William Wordsworth, which extolled the Yarrow River in County Selkirk, Scotland.

Yellepit, YEL-uh-pit (Benton). Former town and a way station on the Seattle, Portland and Spokane Railroad was named in honor of a Walla Walla Indian chief who was praised by Lewis and Clark and who received one of their famous Jefferson Medals.

Yelm (Thurston). The place's original Indian name came from the word *chelm,* meaning "heat waves rising from the earth." The Indians believed that the waves were sent by the Great Spirit to make the earth bountiful.

Young Island (Skagit). Named by Wilkes in honor of Ewing Young, an American fur trapper who turned farmer and cattleman after settling in the Oregon Territory in 1883.

Yukon Harbor (Kitsap). In accordance with his custom of assigning associated names to adjacent geographic points, Wilkes linked together two comrades-in-arms of the Tripolitan War of 1805. He named the bay after Commodore Samuel Butler and the island to the north for Capt. William Bainbridge. The bay's name was later changed locally as a reminiscent tie-in to the Alaska-Yukon gold rush.

Zenith (King). So named because of its position at the top of a hill. The residents chose this name after voting down the name of South Des Moines when the community secured its own post office, separate from Des Moines, in the late 1890s.

Zillah, ZIL-uh (Yakima). Named by Walter N. Granger in honor of Miss Zillah Oakes, daughter of T. F. Oakes, who was president of the Northern Pacific Railroad. [*See* Granger; Oakesdale.]

Selected Bibliography

Akrigg, G. P. V. and Helen B. *1001 British Columbia Place Names*. Vancouver, Canada: Discovery Press, 1969.

Anderson, Bern. *Surveyor of the Sea: The Life and Voyages of Captain George Vancouver*. Seattle: University of Washington Press, 1960.

Association of Washington Cities Directory. Seattle: Municipal Research and Services Center of Washington, 1970.

Avery, Mary W. *Washington: A History of the Evergreen State*. Seattle: University of Washington Press, 1965.

Bagley, Clarence B. *History of King County*. Chicago: S. J. Clarke Publishing Co., 1929.

————. *History of Seattle*. Chicago: S. J. Clarke Publishing Co., 1916.

Ballard, Robert. *Coastal Exploration of Washington*. Palo Alto, Calif.: Pacific Books, 1959.

Book of Counties. N.p.: Washington State Association of County Commissioners and Engineers, 1953.

Cheney, Robert Carkeek. "Montana Place Names," *Montana Magazine* 20, no. 1 (1970).

Cleveland High School. *The Duwamish Diary, 1884–1949*. Seattle: Seattle Public Schools, 1949.

Cook, Fred S., and Hardy, Barlow. *Washington State Travel Book*. Yakima, Wash.: Franklin Press, 1962.

Dryden, Cecil. *Dryden's History of Washington*. Portland, Ore.: Binfords and Mort, 1968.

Edson, Lelah Jackson. *The Fourth Corner: Highlights from the Early Northwest*. Bellingham, Wash.: Cox Brothers, 1951.

Eells, Myron. "Aboriginal Geographic Names in the State of Washington," *American Anthropologist* 5 (January 1892): 27–35.

Fuller, George W. *A History of the Pacific Northwest.* New York: Alfred A. Knopf, 1966.

Gudde, Erwin G. *California Place Names.* Berkeley: University of California Press, 1969.

Hanford, C. H. *Seattle and Environs, 1852–1924.* Chicago: Pioneer Historical Publishing Co., 1924.

Hult, Ruby El. *The Untamed Olympics.* Portland: Binfords and Mort, 1954.

Kellogg, George Albert. *A History of Whidbey's Island.* N.p.: Island County Historical Society, 1934.

Kirk, Ruth. *Exploring Mount Rainier.* Seattle: University of Washington Press, 1968.

———. *Exploring the Olympic Peninsula.* Seattle: University of Washington Press, 1964.

Laufer, Harold. *State Golden Jubilee Report of the County Road Engineer.* Seattle: King County, 1939.

Landes, Henry. *A Geographic Dictionary of Washington.* Washington Geological Survey, Bulletin No. 17, 1917.

McArthur, Lewis A. *Oregon Geographic Names.* Portland, Ore.: Binfords and Mort, 1965.

McCurdy, James G. *By Juan de Fuca's Strait.* Portland, Ore.: Binfords and Mort, 1937.

McDonald, Lucille. *Coast Country.* Portland, Ore.: Binfords and Mort, 1966.

———. *Search for the Northwest Passage.* Portland, Ore.: Binfords and Mort, 1958.

———. *Washington's Yesterdays.* Portland, Ore.: Binfords and Mort, 1935.

Meany, Edmond S. *Mount Rainier: A Record of Exploration.* Portland, Ore.: Binfords and Mort, 1916.

———. *Origin of Washington Geographic Names.* Seattle: University of Washington Press, 1923.

———. *Vancouver's Discovery of Puget Sound.* New York: MacMillan, 1907.

Middleton, Lynn. *Place Names of the Pacific Northwest Coast.* Seattle: Superior Publishing Co., 1969.

Morgan, C. T. *The San Juan Story.* Friday Harbor, Wash.: San Juan Industries, 1966.

Ramsey, Guy Reed. *Postmarked Washington: Okanogan County*. Ephrata, Wash.: Okanogan County Historical Society, 1966.

Ross, Alexander. *Adventures of the First Settlers on the Oregon or Columbia River*. Ed. Milo Milton Quaife. New York: The Citadel Press, 1969.

Rundell, Hugh A. *Washington Names: A Pronunciation Guide*. 2nd ed.; Pullman: Washington State University, 1960[?].

Sainsbury, George, and Hertzog, Nanci. *The Dam Book*. Mercer Island, Wash.: Klatawa Enterprises, 1970.

Schoenberg, Wilfred P., S.J. *A Chronicle of Catholic History of the Pacific Northwest 1743–1960*. Portland, Ore.: Catholic Sentinel Printery, 1962.

Shaw, George C. *The Chinook Jargon*. Seattle: Rainier Printing Co., 1909.

Spencer, Lloyd, and Pollard, Lancaster. *A History of the State of Washington*. New York: American Historical Society, 1937.

Stewart, George R. *American Place-Names*. New York: Oxford University Press, 1970.

———. *Names on the Land*. Boston: Houghton Mifflin, 1967.

Swanton, John R. *Indian Tribes of the Pacific Northwest*. Smithsonian Institution, Bureau of American Ethnology, Bulletin 145. Reprint— Seattle: Shorey Book Store, 1965.

Works Project Administration. *Washington: A Guide to the Evergreen State*. Portland, Ore.: Binfords and Mort, 1941.